A Worship—Filled Life

A Worship-Filled Life

Marcos Witt

CREATION HOUSE
Orlando, FL

A WORSHIP-FILLED LIFE by Marcos Witt
Published by Creation House
Strang Communications Company
600 Rinehart Road
Lake Mary, Florida 32746
Web site: http://www.creationhouse.com

Unless otherwise noted, all Scripture quotations are from the
Holy Bible, New International Version. Copyright © 1973,
1978; 1984, International Bible Society. Used by permission.

Scripture quotations marked KJV are from the King
James Version of the Bible.

Scripture quotations marked NKJV are from the New King
James Version of the Bible. Copyright © 1979, 1980, 1982
by Thomas Nelson, Inc., publishers. Used by permission.

Previously published as *Adoremos*, copyright © 1993,
by Editorial Caribe y distrubuido por Editorial Betania.
ISBN: 0-88113-195-4

Library of Congress Cataloging-in-Publication Data
Witt, Marcos.
A worship-filled life / Marcos Witt.
    p. cm.
  ISBN 0-88419-543-0
  1. God—worship and love.   2. Praise of God.   I. Title.
BV4817.W58 1998
248.3—dc21   98-27146
                                                CIP

8 9 0 1 2 3 4 5 BBG 8 7 6 5 4 3 2 1
Printed in the United States of America

Worship is
the missing jewel
in modern evangelicalism.
We're organized, we work,
we have our agencies. We have
almost everything, but there's one thing
that the churches, even the gospel churches,
do not have: that is the ability to worship.
We are not cultivating the art of worship. It is
the shining gem that is lost to the modern
church, and I believe that we should
search for it until we find it.

—*A. W. Tozer*

Acknowledgments

Miriam—thanks for standing with me during the long days that were involved in committing these thoughts to writing. You are truly a soldier of the Lord. I never cease to be amazed at your grace. Thanks for being such a loving support in everything God has called us to do.

Elena, Jonathan, Kristofer, and Carlos—you guys are the best kids a dad could have. Your mom and I have always prayed that the Lord will turn you into powerful voices for your generation. Thanks for starting that by praying for Dad and standing with me every time I minister to the people.

A special word of thanks goes out to my colaborers and coworkers in the Lord—all the people who make up CanZion, Mas Que Musica, and CCDMAC. Thanks for working with us to build the kingdom of heaven.

Jim Cook—the man who first believed in this missionary kid as a writer. I'll never forget you, Jim, no matter where you go or what you do. I owe you an eternal debt of gratitude for everything your friendship has meant to me over the years.

Jeannie Theo—you're the best! Thanks for your hours and hours of dedication to get this work done in English. You did a great job. I know you did it because of your commitment to building the kingdom of God. That makes what you did even more special.

Tessie Devore—I not only value you as one of our dearest friends, but I admire the way you give everything you have to build the kingdom. David, you're a blessed man; your wife is a treasure to the body of Christ in Latin America. Thanks, Tess.

Esteban Strang—thanks for your encouragement, your friendship, the golf times together, and the words of counsel and wisdom. I'm honored to be a very small part of the vision the Lord has given you. Thanks for believing in me.

Tom Freiling and everybody at Creation House—I'm honored to be one of your authors. My prayer is that the Lord will use this book to mobilize people to worship Him. Let's make it our goal.

And to You, Lord Jesus—what would we do without You? Where would we be without You? You are the reason for everything I do: the songs I sing, the trips I make, and anything else I do. I honor You and worship You. I want to be more like You. I want to be a true worshiper of You. I pray that You will teach us Your ways so that we may know You more. I want to know Your heart and do everything as You do it. I love You.

Contents

One
Thanksgiving 1

Two
Praise 19

Three
Before Becoming a Worshiper 35

Four
Worship 55

Five
Why Is There a Shortage of True Worshipers? 71

Six
An Encounter With God 83

Seven
The Importance of Praising and Worshiping 101

Eight
Those Who Dwell in Zion 111

Nine
When We All Get to Heaven 125

Ten
Common Problems in Praise and Worship 143

Conclusion 159

Notes 161

When we place our trust in Christ,
we can walk the highway of assurance,
knowing that "in [the middle of] everything"
we can give thanks, assured in the knowledge
that He is working His perfect will.

One

Phase I (handwritten)

Thanksgiving - Attitude

W E NEED TO LEARN HOW TO ENTER INTO THE PRESENCE OF the Lord. I don't mean to sound as if He is some-where "out there," some place where we need to go. The Lord is omnipresent; we don't have to go anywhere to be able to be in His presence.

The phrase *enter in,* as used throughout this study, is meant to help us understand that although He is in every place, He's not recognized in every place and given the opportunity to work. For example, if we think about being in the supermarket or mall, truly He is in every one of those places. However, until He is recognized and given the opportunity, He cannot move in our lives. To "come into His presence" does not refer to a physical place to which we need to go, but a place of recognition and sur-render to His will.

The first phase of coming into His presence and al-lowing Him to move in our lives has to do with an attitude

1

of thanksgiving. This will be our starting place.

> Enter his gates with thanksgiving
>> and his courts with praise;
>> give thanks to him and praise his name.
>> —PSALM 100:4

This psalm invites us to come into the holy of holies where the presence of the Lord abides. There is a protocol, if you will, a correct manner in which the priests came before the Lord. This psalm refers to the tabernacle of Moses where the ark of the covenant containing the presence of God rested. If we study the scriptures relating to the tabernacle of Moses, we can get a clearer picture of what the Lord requires of believers, as priests, in order to come into the place where His presence resides. There is only one way to come into the presence of the Lord, and that is through the "gates" of thanksgiving.

One of my Bible school teachers said, "The level of your thankfulness is directly related to your level of spirituality." At first his declaration sounded a little radical to me. But the more I thought about it, the more it made sense. How can we call ourselves "spiritual" or "committed" to the Lord if we are ungrateful to Him? Taken to a completely different level, let me ask the following question: Isn't it true that a person's level of gratefulness has a lot to do with determining his or her emotional state? One who is at odds with everyone is often exercising an ungrateful attitude. Unfortunately, many times our ungratefulness is even directed toward the Lord. An ungrateful heart will most definitely affect our relationship with Him.

Thankfulness plays an important part in helping us to become true worshipers. James says that it's impossible for sweet and bitter water to come from the same fountain (James 3:8–12). If this is true, then it is impossible to be a true worshiper, rendering true praise (sweet water), and be ungrateful (bitter water) at the same time. This condition in our lives must be corrected before going any further in our quest to become a true worshiper.

UNGRATEFULNESS

LET'S TAKE A LOOK AT WHAT PAUL WRITES TO TIMOTHY:

> But mark this: There will be terrible times in the last days. People will be . . . ungrateful.
> —2 TIMOTHY 3:1–2

It is interesting to note that in a list of many unacceptable attitudes, the apostle includes ungratefulness as a sign of two things: "terrible times" and "the last days."

If we were to choose any one word that could describe the attitude of most people these days, I think it would have to be the word *ungrateful.* Everyone seems to be preoccupied with his or her own interests, needs, and desires and has no time for the needs, hurts, and afflictions of others. As we listen to people around us, one gets the distinct feeling that most people today think that society "owes" them something. They live with the mind-set of people waiting to be given something, instead of being people who are looking for opportunities to *give* to others. When they do receive something, instead of saying "thank you," they may say: "Well, it's about time you gave me something," or "It sure took you a while to get this to me."

This unfortunate "gimme" attitude is one of the contributing factors to the breakdown of the moral fiber of our society. We haven't found that place of "contentment." We always want more, and when we can't have it we begin accusing everything and everyone for not having what we think we "deserve." Then we start transferring the responsibility for meeting our needs to others. This is a very advanced stage of ungratefulness.

The following scriptures give us advice we need to remember:

Keep your lives free from the love of money and be content with what you have.

—HEBREWS 13:5

But if we have food and clothing, we will be content with that.

—1 TIMOTHY 6:8

The dictionary defines the word *ungrateful* as "not thankful for favors; disagreeable; thankless." The first part of this definition stirred me when I read it. How quickly we forget the favors we have received from the Lord— His love, mercy, and grace. It's so easy to forget! We get busy with our everyday life, our responsibilities, and thousands of other things, and we forget all the benefits and blessings of the Lord. No wonder the psalmist says, " . . . and forget not all his benefits" (Ps. 103:2). The psalmist David realized that gratefulness is an important ingredient in the life of a worshiper. It is a very happy day in the life of the believer when we come to the realization that the Lord has given us "every good and perfect gift" (James 1:17). We can be "content" with what we have—it's good and perfect.

Satisfied, grateful living reflects our gratitude and brings us into a dimension of peace as nothing else can. I challenge you to seek that place of contentment.

A few years ago I had the "bug" to buy a new vehicle; I thought the one I had was no longer useful for the purposes of the kingdom. (I'm sure I'm not the only one who has found excuses to blame the Lord for not fulfilling our personal desires.) I found myself saying these things: "Lord, you know that I want to serve You. But this car is old, and it prevents me from serving You the best that I can. If You want to keep counting on my help to build Your kingdom, You're just going to have to come through with a new one."

I went so far as to specify what *kind* of new car I wanted:

"Lord, it needs to be this year's model, forest green, with air conditioning, power steering, and all the extras."

During that time I would look at everyone else's car while driving down the street or freeway, dreaming about having one like some of the new cars I saw. My discontent reached such a height about this one thing that my whole life became one of ungratefulness to the Lord. I would pray: "Lord, how is it possible that You bless the unrighteous more than Your servants? How do You expect me to serve You well if You don't give me adequate tools with which to do the job?"

One day while driving on one of the freeways in the United States I heard the Lord say something to me. "Marcos, how fast are you going?"

I answered, "Excuse me, Lord, but does that have anything to do with what we were talking about?"

The Lord responded, "It has everything to do with it."

"Well, Lord," I answered, "I'm going . . . (I paused to slow down.) Now I'm going the speed limit. Why, Father?"

The Lord answered me again, but in His characteristic way, He did so softly, without a lot of fanfare, coming straight to the point. "I don't see you walking down this freeway or broken down on the side of the road. Even if you were, remember that I am always with you, and I will never leave you or forsake you. You have a car that gets you around well (even at speeds above the speed limit), it's paid for, and all you have to do is put gasoline in it and make these trips. You've never lacked for food and clothing or a place to sleep. What are you complaining about?" And then, as quickly as He had begun speaking to me, He stopped.

But did I ever get the message! I started singing and praising Him and thanking Him for His continual gifts of incredible love and grace. I looked at my car and was able to see it through eyes of appreciation and gratefulness. It had been a gift from the Lord, given to me on an earlier occasion by some friends.

GRATITUDE AS AN OFFERING

NEARLY ALL OF THE OLD TESTAMENT OFFERINGS AND SACRIFICES contained an element of "thanksgiving." When the Israelites offered a sacrifice, they did not do it only to ask forgiveness for sins, but also to give thanks that they were still alive to be able to do it. There was a general recognition of the great, powerful, and fearsome God they served. They were not merely acting in obedience to God's commands when they made a sacrifice, but also in gratitude to God for allowing them to continue to live and be able to draw near to Him.

One of the offerings the Israelites gave regularly was the "peace offering" (Lev. 7:11–12, KJV). One of the reasons for giving this offering was as "an expression of thankfulness" (v. 12). Several verses speak about the offering of thanksgiving. (See Leviticus 22:29; Psalm 50:14; 107:22; 116:17; Amos 4:5; Jonah 2:9).

I think the idea of offering a sacrifice is very interesting with this application. The dictionary talks about a *sacrifice* as "the offering of something precious to deity." Another interesting definition is "to accept the loss or destruction of, for an end, cause, or ideal." Still another definition is "loss, deprivation."

The definition in the Spanish dictionary has an added punch to it. I want to share it with you: "voluntary effort or action imposed upon oneself." I like this definition because it speaks of the fact that a sacrifice is something that doesn't come *naturally*. We must impose it upon ourselves; it is an act of the will. Many people *act* grateful only when they *feel* grateful, but the idea of a sacrifice widens our view to include the offering up of gratefulness as a sacrifice or a voluntary action that we impose on ourselves to show our gratitude to the Lord—even when we don't *feel* like it.

One of the Hebrew words that mean "thanksgiving" is

the word *towdah.* This word has three basic meanings: 1) to give praise to God, 2) confession, and 3) a sacrifice of thanksgiving. The Scriptures support this idea of a relationship between sacrifice and thanksgiving.

> Sacrifice thank offerings to God.
>
> —PSALM 50:14

> Through Jesus, therefore, let us continually offer to God a sacrifice of praise—the fruit of lips that confess his name.
>
> —HEBREWS 13:15

The sacrifice of thanksgiving goes hand in hand with praise to the Lord. Our thanks to the Lord should be part of what we offer to the Lord as a premeditated, prepared offering, a voluntary action imposed upon ourselves. It is not just something we do casually or "on the run." We should make a commitment to offer thanksgiving as a sacrifice to Him.

Leviticus 22:29 says, "When you sacrifice a thank offering to the LORD, sacrifice it in such a way that it will be accepted on your behalf." In this example, along with the concept of our thank offering being a sacrifice to the Lord, there's the added element of making sure it's an *acceptable* offering. This indicates that our heart's motivation must be correct when we offer our sacrifice of thanks.

Giving a sacrifice of thanksgiving needn't be something arduous, boring, or annoying; in fact, *thanks giving* should become our lifestyle. When you meditate on all the wonderful things the Lord has created, not only in His eternal creation but also in our daily lives, it is impossible to be an ungrateful person. Yet thanks giving is so hard for us! Most of us find it much easier to complain about everything that is happening around us than to be grateful for it. Every day we should remind ourselves, "This is the day the LORD has made; let us rejoice and be glad in it" (Ps. 118:24). If we do, then it won't be so difficult to give thanks during that day.

It is sometimes hard to understand that we are to give thanks in *everything*. Paul instructed the Thessalonians: "Give thanks in all circumstances" (1 Thess. 5:18). Paul makes it even more challenging by adding: " . . . for this is God's will for you in Christ Jesus." Many of us are seeking the will of God for our lives. Why, then, do we fail to give thanks in all circumstances—when it has been clearly revealed as His will? There is no need to continue looking for more of His will until we have done what He already told us to do—don't you agree?

This is such a simple yet complicated commandment. I wish it could be as easy as saying, "Lord, thanks for everything . . . " and that would be the end of it. But it's not. For some reason it's very hard for us to be a grateful people.

It is true that it's harder to give thanks when things aren't going well, when we feel as if the world is closing in upon us. When things aren't going well we struggle with questions like these: "Do I have to give thanks when a loved one dies? How can I be thankful when I lose my job? How can I give thanks when my children run away from home and my husband comes home drunk every night?"

If we could learn to give thanks *in* everything, we would become true worshipers. Give thanks *in spite* of what happens. Give thanks *in the middle* of what happens. It is hard—yes, impossible—to understand all the Lord is doing or will do through difficult circumstances in our lives. But the confidence we have in Him and the intimate relationship we've nurtured with Him over the years pay off in our thanks giving. One thing we know for sure: "All things work together for good to those who love God, to those who are the called according to His purpose" (Rom. 8:28, NKJV). We've proven it to be true over and over.

In the Book of John we find the story of Lazarus's death, a man who was a close friend of Jesus. (See John 11.) Yet, in spite of their close relationship, when Jesus received the news of His friend's grave illness, even unto death, He calmly continued His work where He was—without seeming to give the news about Lazarus much notice. He said something to His disciples about the illness being "for God's glory," and then He informed them that He would be traveling to Judea—not to Bethany where Lazarus lived.

What a strange way for the Lord to do things! Most of us would have run to our friend's bedside to pray, intercede, and do whatever we could to comfort him. But Jesus, who has "global vision"—the ability to see all the things we cannot see—calmly went about His business.

It's very easy today for us to read that story and know what is going to happen. But let's put ourselves in the shoes of Mary and Martha, Lazarus's sisters. They knew that Jesus had the power to heal their brother. That's why, when he fell gravely ill, they sent for Jesus, saying, "Lord, we need You to come as quickly as possible because our brother, Lazarus, is at the point of death, and we need a miracle." I can imagine that the sisters could hardly wait to hear Jesus' response when the messenger returned. How disappointed they must have been to find that He hadn't even told them when He would come. All the messenger could tell them was that Jesus had turned to His disciples, told them the illness was "for God's glory," and then said, "Let's go to Judea, guys!"

Can you imagine how disconcerted these two sisters must have felt upon hearing this terrible news? Can you feel the frustration they must have experienced, knowing that apparently the Lord didn't even care about their beloved brother's problem?

Isn't it true that many times you have felt the same way when asking something of the Lord? Isn't it true that many times we lament our "horrible" situation and ask the Lord, "Why have You abandoned me?" Like Mary and Martha when they knew the Lord was not coming, we feel as though He doesn't care about what's happening. What a cause for desperation! What a good reason for not giving thanks!

Four days later, things got worse—Lazarus died and was buried (that was the end of hoping to see their brother healed). Everyone returned home, grieving and lamenting the loss of their beloved brother and friend, Lazarus. That's when Jesus showed up—four days "late." Immediately, the two sisters ran to meet Him, just as we would have done—not with thanksgiving but with complaints and protests: "Lord, if you had been here, my brother would not have died" (vv. 21, 32).

You may say that's a *natural* complaint for someone in those circumstances. But the Word is trying to teach us how to become *supernatural*. To be supernatural, we must learn from the Word that even in the midst of life-and-death circumstances, such as those facing Lazarus and his sisters, we can give a sacrifice (voluntary effort) of thanks. In fact, the very circumstances that, in the natural, meant defeat for Lazarus, the Lord took and made them work for good. We must learn to trust in Him, rest in Him, and know that He has everything under control.

Jesus cried when He met the grieving sisters. I believe He cried for several reasons. One reason was because He saw so much unbelief around Him. Everyone was thinking, *If only He had arrived sooner. What a shame that He didn't care earlier about what was going on. If He could heal others, He could have healed Lazarus.*

To Martha Jesus said, "Did I not tell you that if you believed, you would see the glory of God?" (v. 40). We can almost hear His admonishment: "Don't doubt; believe." The Lord is saddened when we fail to have a heart that trusts His will or when we prefer to walk the path of unbelief. When we place our trust in Christ, we can walk the highway of assurance, knowing that "in [the middle of] everything" we can give thanks, assured in the knowledge that He is working His perfect will.

In the end, everything happened exactly as Jesus had planned—resulting in a supernatural display of the glory of God. During these events, I think Mary and Martha learned a valuable lesson: If you believe, you will see the glory of God. Will we be able to learn this lesson for ourselves? We can move forward on our way to becoming true worshipers by changing this area of our lives and learning to obey the truth of 1 Thessalonians 5:18: "Give thanks in all circumstances, for this is God's will for you."

It is a very hard challenge, but one we need to take if we want to know our Lord more intimately. I invite you to take a minute to thank the Lord *in the midst* of whatever circumstance you may be going through right now. Don't put this off, because to become a grateful person you must begin being grateful *right now*. Right there where you are, begin to think of all the things the Lord has done for you. Admit that you cannot understand the unfathomable ways of God. With your finite understanding of things, show Him your trust by giving an offering or sacrifice of thanksgiving. Do it in an audible voice—it doesn't matter who's around you. Begin to give thanks in the middle of that circumstance you're going through. I believe with all my heart, and I'll declare it to you, that at this very moment you are beginning a new lifestyle. From now on, you will be a more grateful person than you were before.

A LIFESTYLE

HAVE YOU KNOWN SOMEONE WHO SPENDS ALL HIS OR HER TIME complaining? That person may have permanent creases in his forehead because he spends so much time frowning. He may even look disagreeable, angry, and frustrated.

Other people seem to be living the "golden years" of their lives with a constant smile. They're always happy, and they laugh at everything. Have you noticed the wrinkles they have? They are smile wrinkles—wrinkles caused by happiness and joy.

I had a beautiful grandmother who reached old age with wonderful wrinkles on her face. She was a woman acquainted with pain, suffering, and hard times. Her husband, my grandfather, a headstrong man with lots of passion, had a healthy dose of "wanderlust." Papa Witt told me once that he and his wife had lived in at least fifty different cities during their lifetimes.

It had not been an easy life for my grandmother. She buried two of her three children during her lifetime. The first one (my father) died when he was barely twenty-one years old. Her other son died at forty-three years of age. My grandmother had such a wonderful relationship with God. In all my life, I never heard one single word of ingratitude come out of her mouth, nor one of protest or doubt.

She was a person characterized by her beautiful smile, her happy disposition, and her personality, which wasn't frivolous but could still enjoy hearing and telling a good joke. Her laughter was as contagious as her optimism. I was present at my uncle Tim's (who was her youngest child) funeral in 1990. I knew that this had been a hard blow to her, and I watched her draw strength from the fountain of living waters. I was amazed at her manner of speaking to the Lord during that difficult moment. The way she related to the Lord was so intimate, so confident. Suddenly I knew how she got all those smile wrinkles on her forehead—she knew the Lord!

She had a confidence that whatever God was doing in her life was perfect. This confidence brought her a peace and joy beyond what the *normal* person has. She had developed a lifestyle of giving thanks in everything—it had become part of her very nature. She didn't have to tell herself consciously: *Okay, now I have to be thankful because this is the will of God for my life.* She simply did it as a result of knowing God.

Have you realized the urgency of your need to get to know God in this same way? Begin right now. Make the decision to change and to allow the Holy Spirit to mold your heart so that "giving thanks in everything" becomes a part of your very nature—your lifestyle.

The psalmist David was a man who set goals for himself. Let's look at some of his goals:

> I will praise God's name in song
> and glorify him with thanksgiving [*towdah*].
> —PSALM 69:30

> I will sacrifice a thank offering [*towdah*].
> —PSALM 116:17

One of the interesting things about David's writing is the decisive way in which he expresses himself: "I *will* praise . . . I *will* glorify . . . I *will* sacrifice. . . . " These are all declarations that show us a little of David's character. He was a man of resolve, determination, and purpose. He set goals and reached them. Giving thanks (*towdah*) was a part of his nature, a part of his being, a part of his lifestyle. He lived in a constant state of gratitude.

Another Hebrew word the psalmist often uses in his writings, *yadah*, means "thanksgiving," but it has a slightly different connotation. *Yadah* also means "to fall or throw down." I believe this is indicative of bowing. It is giving thanks by bowing down before the throne of the Lord in reverence and respect for all that He has done and will do for us. We will talk more about bowing in a later chapter, but right now I want us to look at a few places where David uses the word *yadah* in his writings. In each instance, note his tone of voice as he writes—it is one of determination . . . resolve . . . no questions asked—it is part of his lifestyle.

> . . . that my heart may sing to you and not be silent.

13

O LORD my God, I will give you thanks [*yadah*] forever.

—PSALM 30:12

I will give you thanks in the great assembly;
among the throngs of people I will praise [*yadah*]
you.

—PSALM 35:18

Therefore I will praise [*yadah*] you among the
nations, O LORD;
I will sing praises to your name.

—PSALM 18:49

Each one of these passages teaches us to determine to
be grateful people. The last passage uses another aspect
of *yadah*, that of "confessing." This is one of the definitions of the word *yadah*, and in the Spanish translation
the word *confess* is used in this scripture. It reads, "I will
confess You among the nations."

There is no doubt that as we bow before the Lord (not
necessarily a physical bowing, but a lifestyle), our lives
and our testimonies are witnesses "among the nations" to
a living, powerful, awesome, wonderful God who dwells
among His people.

It's time to put the ingredient of thanksgiving into our
daily lives. We will be much more confident, sure, and
stable with the knowledge that even though we do not
know all the Lord is doing with and through us, we do
know His will is being fulfilled in our lives. Therefore, we
can be grateful in the midst of everything that happens to us.

HOMEWORK

LET ME LEAVE YOU WITH A HOMEWORK ASSIGNMENT. THIS EXERCISE
helped me to check the level of gratitude in my life. May
it do the same in yours. On a sheet of paper, make three

columns titled "Spirit," "Soul," and "Body" respectively.

List the things for which you are thankful under each heading. For example, good health would go under the "Body" heading; love for your children would go under "Soul"; and the spirit of gratefulness that the Lord is working into your life would go under the heading of "Spirit," since it is something being developed in that part of your being.

Then take some time to analyze the areas where you are less grateful. Ask God to help you to be more grateful in those areas.

This simple exercise will allow you to see, in writing, your weak areas as far as gratefulness is concerned, and it will give you an opportunity to strengthen them on your way to becoming a true worshiper.

AN ATTITUDE OF GRATITUDE

AN ATTITUDE OF GRATEFULNESS IS A CHARACTERISTIC FOUND IN THE life of a true worshiper. We can discover this fact in the following passages:

> The LORD will surely comfort Zion
>   and will look with compassion on all her ruins;
> he will make her deserts like Eden,
>   her wastelands like the garden of the LORD.
> Joy and gladness will be found in her,
>   thanksgiving and the sound of singing.
>
> —ISAIAH 51:3

> Now he who supplies seed to the sower and bread for food will also supply and increase your store of seed and will enlarge the harvest of your righteousness. You will be made rich in every way so that you can be generous on every occasion, and through us your generosity will result in thanksgiving to God.
>
> —2 CORINTHIANS 9:10–11

15

. . . rooted and built up in him, strengthened in the faith as you were taught, and overflowing with thankfulness.

—COLOSSIANS 2:7

Do you still want to be a true worshiper? Now that we have learned how to be a grateful person, we can go on to the next step in becoming a true worshiper: the step of praise.

Praise is seldom silent.
We have a cause to celebrate,
Someone to boast about,
and a victory to declare—
why do it in silence?
Let's tell the whole world.

Two

Praise

THE LONGER WE LIVE THE MORE WE LEARN ABOUT THE WAY God thinks, His nature, and His character through the things and persons the Lord puts near us. For example, when my wife and I had the honor of becoming parents for the first time, our whole life changed. Children are the best teachers; when you become a parent many things are revealed to you of which you were ignorant before.

That's one of the reasons the Lord told His disciples, "I tell you the truth, unless you change and become like little children, you will never enter the kingdom of heaven" (Matt. 18:3). On another occasion, He said to the teachers, "Have you never read, 'From the lips of children and infants you have ordained praise'?" (Matt. 21:16).

One of the best examples I can use to illustrate the difference between praise and worship is one I see every day when I come home. When my children hear me open the front door, a shout can be heard all throughout the

19

house: "Daddy, Daddy . . . Yeah! Daddy's home!" Kids come running from every which way to hug my legs, to celebrate, to jump, and shout simply because of the fact that I'm home. My wife and I have four children. When this celebration begins, I usually have all four of them on me at the same time. Invariably, one will be on my shoulders, another hanging off one of my arms, and the other two hugging me, kissing me, or all of the above.

These outward expressions of my childrens' inner feelings of admiration, love, and rejoicing are a natural response upon seeing the one they love. No one "taught" them how to express this; it's something that was birthed in them by God.

As I take them in my arms and tell them how much I love them, they begin telling me that they love me, and they shower me with kisses. Then something happens. Their tone of voice changes; their words, formerly of rejoicing, now become loving and intimate. They say things like: "Daddy, I love you so much. . . . You're the best dad in the whole world. . . . You're the most handsome dad." Phrases like that are music to a loving parent's ears. Through this simple illustration we can see a basic difference between praise (celebration) and worship (intimacy).

When our heavenly Father arrives, our *natural* reaction is one of rejoicing, celebration, and praise. Someone we love has arrived. Someone who means *everything* to us. Our reaction to Him is the same as my children's reaction to my return home. But once we've drawn near to Him, had the privilege of being taken in His arms of love, and have received His caresses, the celebration changes to worship. In worship we have the opportunity to tell Him our deepest, most intimate thoughts. To do this, one doesn't need to make a lot of noise. On the contrary, it's often necessary to speak softly, tenderly, and lovingly in order to make the most of the close communion we are enjoying with Him at that moment.

For many years it was thought that praise and worship were the same thing. Now the Lord has been leading us into the understanding that they are two different things. We must learn how to discern the time we spend with Him, whether in praise or in worship, so that our relationship can be whole and complete. The Bible speaks of the difference between these two things time and time again. In this chapter we want to study about *praise:* the naturally festive reaction to the arrival of our Lord among us, or of our "arrival" (coming) before Him.

PRAISE IS A PARTY!

PSALM 100 TELLS US:

> Shout for joy to the LORD, all the earth.
> Worship the LORD with gladness;
> come before him with joyful songs.
>
> —VERSES 1–2

The Hebrew words used in this passage are *ruwa* ("shout for joy"), which means "shout, raise a sound, cry out, give a blast," and *renanah* ("joyful songs"), which means "shout of joy, joyful voice, singing, triumphing, and ringing cry." It's interesting that in this passage we are ordered to draw near to God with loud and festive rejoicing.

In his book *The Practice of Praise,* Don McMinn says: " . . . praise should be more like a party than a funeral."[1] Many of us have erroneously thought that coming before the Lord with joy and celebration is synonymous with irreverence. Yet the Bible not only teaches us that this is the way to draw near to God; it *orders* it. As we have heard said many times, "God does not give suggestions, only commandments."

Psalm 145:3 says, "Great is the LORD and most worthy of praise." In my Spanish Bible, this scripture reads: "Great is the LORD and worthy of *supreme* praise" (emphasis

21

added). The word *supreme* says a lot to me: He is worthy of my *best* praise; He is worthy of the highest praise. When I see the word *supreme*, I can't think of a greater way to praise Him. One of the synonyms for this word is *paramount;* it is the highest way of worshiping the Lord. The praise we offer to the Lord should be higher than any we would offer to some person, institution, or entity. It should be expressed with such submission, energy, and devotion that there is no doubt as to what we are doing.

The Bible speaks a lot about celebrations. In fact, the Lord established seven different celebrations that were observed throughout the year. Some of them were annual; others took place monthly or weekly. The Hebrew word for celebration is *chagag,* and it means "have a party; have a festival or a procession; celebrate; dance."

In the parable of the prodigal son, Jesus shows the heart of the Father to be patient, loving, and full of mercy. There is an obvious comparison between the earthly father of this lost son and our heavenly Father. When the son finally returns, far from rejecting him, the father receives him, dresses him, and returns to him the prestige and honor of the family name. The father puts a ring on the returning son's finger, a sign of familial authority. But the icing on the cake is when the father arranges to kill the fatted calf, bringing musicians and people from near and far, throwing a huge "welcome home" party.

It wasn't a quiet little affair, because we know the older brother could hear the racket from afar off. Even before entering the house, he knew something special was happening, and he asked what was going on (Luke 15:25–26). The heart of this earthly father—and that of our heavenly Father—rejoices in His children, and He likes to celebrate their repentance with them.

In 1986, Mexico was the host country for the World Cup of soccer. My wife and I were newlyweds, and we lived next door to some young guys who loved to watch soccer. We had become friends with some of them, and we found ourselves watching some of the matches together on television.

I remember the first match of the competition: Mexico played Belgium in the impressive Aztec Stadium, filled to capacity that day with more than one hundred twenty thousand people attending, including the president of Mexico and other dignitaries of the Mexican government. After the opening ceremonies there was a short speech by the president, a salute to the flag, and the playing of the national anthem; after all the protocol, the game began.

I don't remember details about the game, but I do know that I yelled a lot while cheering on the Mexican team, hoping they would make the first goal of the World Cup, which they did. In one unforgettable moment, the ball made its way into the goal. The TV announcer yelled wildly at the top of his lungs: "Go-o-oa-a-lll, go-o-oa-a-lll! Mexico makes the first goal of World Cup 1986!" All the people in the stadium jumped to their feet, hands in the air, shouting and celebrating this group of men who had just made a goal. I saw many grab each other's hands and hug one another; many were in tears. Others threw their hats, caps, or whatever else they had in the air, in a great moment of exhilaration. An atmosphere of wholehearted celebration and festiveness ruled in the entire stadium—and I'm sure in thousands of homes across Mexico and the world—for more than five or ten minutes.

The reality of what was happening came over me strongly—shaking me to the point that I almost felt as if someone had hit me. *These people were praising!* I said to my wife, "Watch this. They are praising. They have their hands raised, they're dancing and shouting (joyfully), and they're celebrating what the players just did." We stood there watching for several minutes, and all of a sudden I didn't feel like celebrating anymore because I realized that the people were giving better praise to the Mexican soccer team than they probably would have given to God Himself.

There have only been a few times when I've seen people burst into praise and celebration to God the way those thousands did in the Aztec Stadium. On the contrary, too many times I've heard all the excuses that can be imagined as to why we should *not* praise the Lord of heaven in that way. This attitude is still a great mystery to me. I have a hard time understanding why we feel it's justifiable to praise sports teams or sports figures with everything we have, but we believe the Son of God shouldn't be praised with the same intensity. Something's wrong with this picture!

Jesus made the biggest goal of all time on Calvary when He triumphed over Satan and made a public spectacle of him, showing all generations the greatness of our God (Col. 2:15). After such a great miracle, how can we *not* dare to give Him the highest of praise? We should have a celebration every day when we remember His work of redemption on the cross and the victory He obtained for us by putting Satan beneath His feet. Ephesians 2:6 tells us that He raised us up in that same victory. Because of that victory, we can walk and live triumphantly every day in the name of Jesus.

There is *no* excuse for not giving Him the best of our celebration praise. We should be the first to shout out His glory because of all the wonderful things He's done for us. Don't hold it back, and don't let anyone tell you we're not supposed to worship Him in that way. Even if we shouted for twenty-four hours nonstop, we still would never be able to repay Him for all His goodness. Let's turn our praise into a real celebration. He not only scored the greatest goal known to man, He won the match!

God created us with certain characteristics in our nature that make us *want* to praise. For example, when someone of whom we have fond memories is mentioned, our natural reaction is to say, "Oh sure, I know him; he is a good friend." We don't think twice about it. Our response pours out of our mouth without even thinking

24

about it. We want to say nice things about people of whom we think well.

By the same token, the mere remembrance of Jesus should elicit a positive, happy, and dynamic response from us. Praise gives us the opportunity to express that happiness in a visible and tangible way. We shout. We lift our hands. We dance. These are outward expressions of our inward love, admiration, and appreciation. Praise allows us to brag on Someone whom we deeply love, which takes us to our next section.

PRAISE IS BOASTING

DID I USE THE WORD *BOAST?* NO, *I* DIDN'T. *THE BIBLE* DID! THE word most used in the Old Testament to speak of praise is the word *halal,* the same root from which the word *hallelujah* comes. On repeated occasions it is used to order praise to God. (See Psalm 22:22–23; 35:18; 56:4; 63:5; 69:30.) The Hebrew word *halal* means "to shine, to show off, celebrate, make much noise and display, be jubilant."

Have you ever seen a young man take the hand of his sweetheart? Watch his face; there's an expression there— almost of pride! Or watch a child who runs out into the street to show off a new toy.

No one who has something good in his life about which he is happy, satisfied, and proud is going to be able to hide it. It's in man's very nature to want to take it out, to show it off, and to talk about it. Why, then, don't Christians, who have such an extraordinarily wonderful God, show Him off so that the whole world can see His eternal love and greatness?

Just as my kids don't worry about "What will Daddy think?" when they meet me so noisily upon my arrival home, so we should be jubilant when we come into the presence of the Lord. Far from being bothered or embarrassed by our praise, He rejoices in the praises of His people. Why have we been so worried about showing the world how wonderful, kind, loving, merciful (and a thousand other attributes) our God is? Don't stop yourself from bragging to as many people as you can about your most *amazing* Lord! This is a testimony to a world that has so few heroes and is constantly making up new ones because the old ones let them down. We have a God that fulfills all of His promises, has never made a mistake, and never has had to apologize to anyone. He is perfect and right in all His ways. This is worth getting excited about—and all the world should know! Don't you agree?

It's time to make our praise a time to boast about all that He means to us. According to the original definition of *halal*, we need to "make Him shine" in this darkened world. Take Him out on the street! Let the neighbors see Him! Talk Him up to all your buddies! It's time for the world to see Jesus as more than a religious figure; it's time for them to see Him as a friend, counselor, Lord, and Savior. The only way the world can know Him as such is through the *halal* of His children.

PRAISE IS WARFARE

DURING THE GULF WAR, THE WORLD BECAME FAMILIAR WITH THE powerful weaponry man has invented to destroy his enemies. The videos being sent back looked almost like science-fiction movies. Taken with cameras attached to the nose of the missiles, they transmitted the signal back to the base and allowed us to see, firsthand, the incredible advances in modern science. The whole world saw the now famous Patriot missile, which could detect the arrival of another missile, intercept the incoming missile, and destroy it with an 85 percent accuracy rate. Wow! The world has gone to great lengths to come up with weapons that can outsmart the enemy and give strategies for winning the war.

There are many parallels in the spiritual realm. The war

that exists in the spiritual world also has a series of ultra-modern and powerful weapons. Paul says, "The weapons we fight with are not the weapons of the world. On the contrary, they have divine power to demolish strongholds" (2 Cor. 10:4). Our war is not carnal, so our weapons cannot be carnal either. The Bible says clearly:

> Our struggle is not against flesh and blood, but against the rulers, against the authorities, against the powers of this dark world and against the spiritual forces of evil in the heavenly realms.
>
> —EPHESIANS 6:12

Why should we use natural weapons such as machine guns, cannons, and rifles when we have access to spiritual atomic bombs of praise, worship, prayer, fasting, and intercession—as well as the Word of God, the blood of the Lamb, and the name of Jesus? Terry Law, in his book *The Power of Praise and Worship*, gives an excellent explanation about these weapons. He says that in all missiles and rockets, the range and power is found in the warhead. If the rocket is not carrying an atomic warhead, then the rocket will only cause local or regional damage at the most. But a missile carrying an atomic warhead becomes the carrier of enormous disaster, destroying entire cities and causing a much greater impact.[2]

Law goes on to say that "the rocket" in this case is *praise*. Praise is merely the carrier of the dangerous warhead. The power is not in the rocket itself, but in the warhead. The atomic warheads are the name of Jesus, the blood of the Lamb, and the Word of God (Rev. 12:11). When we unite the missile of praise with the power of the name, the blood, and the Word, then we can cause serious damage to the enemy's territory. When praise does not carry the atomic warhead it is only music—a simple song with no power.

When we sing, speak, or declare our praise to the

27

Lord, we are letting the opposing side know the powerful eternal truths that are found in the Word. We are pointing and firing at the kingdom of our enemy, reminding him that Jesus has already triumphed over him; therefore we can enjoy the victory He obtained for us.

Fermín García, a well-known Latin American composer, wrote a song titled, *"Majestuoso, Poderoso"* ("Majestic, Powerful"). In this song, Fermín invites us to make resounding and forceful declarations to our enemy. One of the lines in the song reads: "Let us declare His greatness today. Jesus Christ is King, Jesus Christ is King. Bowed now before His feet, we declare that Jesus Christ is King!"[3]

I firmly believe that when Satan hears this declaration coming from the mouth of a believer, he trembles. By saying, "Jesus Christ is King," we are firing a powerful missile into the kingdom of darkness and freeing captives who are under its control. The song itself has no power; it is the carrier of something much more powerful: the declaration found in the Word of God that "Jesus Christ is King."

Before Lucifer's fall from heaven, some say that he was heaven's worship leader. We do know with certainty that he was near the throne of God, because he was called "a guardian cherub" (Ezek. 28:14). Lucifer wanted to be like God—to sit on the throne of God so that all the worship would be directed to him. But God does not share His glory with anyone, and Lucifer was cast out of heaven.

Satan is still trying to take praise and worship for himself, doing everything in his power to get people to bow before him. He was even desirous of receiving praise from the Son of God (Luke 4:5–7). By joining Christ in the resolve to refuse to give Lucifer praise, we throw a little salt into his wounds as we shout to the four winds that "Jesus Christ is King . . . Jesus Christ is the victor . . . Jesus Christ is Lord." These and other similar declarations cause terrible damage to the kingdom of darkness because they are powerfully assertive declarations about the reality of the truth: Jesus is the *winner*; Satan is the *loser*.

Psalm 149:1-6 has always caught my attention because of its unique, and even bizarre, construction. Allow me to explain as we look at it more closely.

> Praise the LORD.
> Sing to the LORD a new song,
>   his praise in the assembly of the saints.
>
> Let Israel rejoice in their Maker;
>   let the people in Zion be glad in their King.
> Let them praise his name with dancing
>   and make music to him with tambourine and harp.
> For the LORD takes delight in his people;
>   he crowns the humble with salvation.
> Let the saints rejoice in this honor
>   and sing for joy on their beds.
> May the praise of God be in their mouths...
>
> —PSALM 149:1–6

Let's pause here for just a moment. Everything is going pretty good in our reading up to now. The psalm is a beautiful piece of writing, inviting us to exalt the Lord and explaining some of the benefits of praise. There are pretty words like: "rejoice," "be glad," "make music," "praise," "the LORD takes delight," "crowns," "sing for joy." These words are wonderful expressions from the heart of the psalmist and show the benefits of our praise. Up to verse 6, we are engrossed in the wonderful thoughts of his writing.

Suddenly his tone changes in the middle of verse 6. The psalmist doesn't even bother to finish the verse before beginning with a totally different thought. He almost interrupts himself as he remembers a powerful aspect of praise: warfare!

> ... and a double-edged sword in their hands,
>   to inflict vengeance on the nations
>   and punishment on the peoples,

29

> to bind their kings with fetters,
> their nobles with shackles of iron,
> to carry out the sentence written against them.
>
> —VERSES 6–9

Then, the writer suddenly changes again as he finishes his psalm:

> This is the glory of all his saints.
> Praise the LORD.
>
> —VERSES 9–10

I don't believe the suddenly shifting style in which this psalm was written was the result of too much pizza the night before the psalmist wrote it. But I do firmly believe that the writer is showing us a powerful truth: Praise affects the kingdom of darkness.

Ephesians 6:12 and 2 Corinthians 10:4 tell us that our struggle is not fought with carnal weapons, but with spiritual ones. One of these weapons, as we've been saying, is praise. When you and I raise our hands in the sanctuary, we are going to war with Satan. When we sing and declare the truths of the eternal Word of God, we are confronting the forces of evil with those truths. When the sounds of our instruments are heard in the kingdom of darkness, they provoke a direct attack on the principalities and powers.

Notice, once more, the words the psalmist uses to describe the effects of our praise: " . . . bind their kings with fetters, their nobles with shackles of iron." Who are the kings and nobles? Aren't they "principalities and powers"? Of course.

The sound of praise that comes out of the mouth and heart of the redeemed of the Lord brings destruction to the kingdom of our enemy. It binds the rulers of darkness, it inflicts the vengeance of the Lord on the workers of injustice, and many other things that our natural eyes can't see—but that our spiritual eyes can.

Isn't it true that a kingdom is a nation? Notice verse 7: " . . . to inflict vengeance on the nations." Our praise inflicts vengeance on the kingdom of Satan.

Psalm 149 was not written in this style by mere chance. On the contrary, it is one of the most powerful psalms showing us the direct relationship between praise and worship and spiritual warfare.

There is another very interesting verse that is found in Isaiah 30:32:

> Every stroke the LORD lays on them
>> with his punishing rod
> will be to the music of tambourines and harps,
>> as he fights them in battle with the blows of his arm.

This verse doesn't say that these strokes will be with man-made bombs, rifles, cannons, or missiles, but that they will be given with music, praise, and worship to God. These are the weapons with which the Lord will fight against them "in battle." The Bible gives many examples of the role of worship in battle. King Jehoshaphat worshiped God when he was surrounded by his enemies. As they went out to battle, his army shouted, "Give thanks to the LORD, for his love endures forever" (2 Chron. 20:22). Joshua and his army brought down the walls of Jericho with a shout of praise (Josh. 6:1–21).

The next time you are in a service praising the Lord, try to remember this principle so that your praise can take on a new perspective and focus. Tell yourself, *As I sing and praise, giving my heart and life to the Lord, I'm bringing more destruction to the kingdom of Satan.* Let yourself praise with even more intensity so as to see all the works of evil destroyed in the spirit. If we remember this, we will want to praise more than ever, and we will do it with more energy and purpose. No wonder the devil doesn't like worshipers—they are bringing him to ruin.

This is why praise is seldom silent. We have a cause to celebrate, Someone to boast about, and a victory to declare—why do it in silence? Let's tell the whole world. Let's lift our voices and make it known that we have a great Lord who has " . . . placed all things under his feet" (Eph. 1:22).

He has given us His victory. AMEN!

We must give Christ the keys
"into" all the areas of our lives
so that His purifying work
can keep us in optimum condition
to serve Him and His body.

Three

Before Becoming a Worshiper

THE LORD IS MORE INTERESTED IN OUR HEART THAN IN ANY other thing. The condition of our heart is a major factor in whether we will become a true worshiper.

Proverbs says, "Above all else, guard your heart, for it is the wellspring of life" (4:23). The dictionary defines the *heart* as "the whole personality; the emotional or moral as distinguished from the intellectual nature; courage; one's innermost being; center; the essential part." To speak of the heart is not to speak of the physical organ that pumps blood throughout the body, but that which is the center of our spiritual existence, just as the physical heart is the center of our natural existence. That is why Proverbs calls it "the wellspring of life." We cannot live without the heart. So, just as we take care of our physical heart, we should take care of our spiritual heart.

It is essential to allow the Lord to penetrate the innermost part of our being so that no areas of our life remain out of His control. The heart is the seat of our being. It is a place hidden to everyone but our own selves. Only we know what is there. No one can guess what man hides in his heart. We may show one thing on the outside, but totally opposite feelings may be lurking on the inside.

Every true worshiper has the need to worship in "truth" (John 4:23)—that is to say, in complete honesty and transparency. Let's take a look at a passage of the Word that helped me to understand the importance of having a heart that is right before God in order to worship Him.

HEZEKIAH RESTORES THE TEMPLE

FOR MANY YEARS I THOUGHT THAT PRAISE AND WORSHIP WERE ONLY outward, physical expressions of gratitude, combined with emotions of happiness and joy to the Lord for all that He represents. Although the outward expression of praise is important, through His Word I began to see that He is more interested in my heart than in my expression of praise.

In many of the praise and worship seminars that I have offered over the years, I have taught from 2 Chronicles 29:26–28:

> So the Levites stood ready with David's instruments, and the priests with their trumpets. Hezekiah gave the order to sacrifice the burnt offering on the altar. As the offering began, singing to the LORD began also, accompanied by trumpets and the instruments of David king of Israel. The whole assembly bowed in worship, while the singers sang and the trumpeters played. All this continued until the sacrifice of the burnt offering was completed.

One day it occurred to me to research the context of this passage in order to know the time in history into which the narrative of this event is positioned. Big surprise! The passage I had always read with such passion in my workshops had an even more profound background that must be considered for a full understanding of what God is saying through this passage.

Let's start at the beginning. Hezekiah was a king who "did what was right in the eyes of the LORD" (2 Chron. 29:2). However, his father, Ahaz, was a perverse man who lived far from God and "walked in the ways of the kings of Israel" (28:2). (In fact, the majority of the kings who ruled after David were perverse, lost, and far from God.) Besides walking in the evil ways of these kings, Ahaz "also made cast idols for worshiping the Baals," which were strange and foreign gods (v. 2).

Not only does history tell us that Ahaz worshiped false gods, but there's yet another interesting detail we can discover. Hezekiah's great-grandfather, Uzziah, began his reign by doing "what was right in the sight of the LORD" (2 Chron. 26:4, NKJV). However, as his pride in his accomplishments grew, he no longer reverenced the house of God. In fact, he "transgressed against the LORD his God by entering the temple of the LORD to burn incense on the altar of incense" (26:16, NKJV). This characteristic of disdain for the house of God passed on to Uzziah's grandson, Ahaz. Ahaz not only disdained the house of the Lord, but he "shut up the doors of the house of the LORD, and made for himself altars in every corner of Jerusalem" (28:24, NJKV).

The temple was the house of God. The sanctuary is the place where God dwells. Today, the New Testament declares that God no longer lives in buildings made by man, but in the hearts of men. (See 2 Corinthians 5:1; cf. 1 Corinthians 3:16–17; 6:19.) Ahaz's disdain for the house of the Lord speaks of a lack of communion with the Lord; this could be one of the main reasons he was so far from God.

There is an important lesson to be learned here. When we neglect our "temple," or when it is scorned, we run the very real risk of becoming distant from God because of our lack of communion with Him. Deep in the heart of every true worshiper there is a need, a longing, an insatiable desire to be in God's house.

David said many things about the Lord's house. Upon reading a few of them, we begin to notice the passion with which he speaks about the Lord's house. As you read, remember that the "house of the Lord" is any place where one has an encounter with God. It can be, but doesn't have to be, a literal building, church, or sanctuary; in our New Testament experience, however, it refers more to having an encounter with God. Consider this:

> One thing I ask of the LORD,
>   this is what I seek:
> that I may dwell in the house of the LORD
>   all the days of my life,
> to gaze upon the beauty of the LORD
>   and to seek him in his temple.
>
> —PSALM 27:4

> . . . and I will dwell in the house of the LORD forever.
>
> —PSALM 23:6

> . . . for zeal for your house consumes me,
>   and the insults of those who insult you fall on me.
>
> —PSALM 69:9

> Better is one day in your courts
>   than a thousand elsewhere;
> I would rather be a doorkeeper in the house of my God
>   than dwell in the tents of the wicked.
>
> —PSALM 84:10

> I rejoiced with those who said to me,
>   "Let us go to the house of the LORD."
>
> —PSALM 122:1

The righteous will flourish like a palm tree,
> they will grow like a cedar of Lebanon;
planted in the house of the LORD,
> they will flourish in the courts of our God.
>> —PSALM 92:12–13

I love the house where you live, O LORD,
> the place where your glory dwells.
>> —PSALM 26:8

Blessed are those you choose
> and bring near to live in your courts!
We are filled with the good things of your house,
> of your holy temple.
>> —PSALM 65:4

Blessed are those who dwell in your house;
> they are ever praising you.
>> —PSALM 84:4

We all have friends with whom we enjoy spending time. My wife and I are blessed to have as some of our closest friends a couple who have four children—just as we do. Between their four and our four, we have a small, noisy army. We enjoy visiting their home for several reasons:

Theirs is a "childproof" home. Those who have children know exactly what I'm talking about. It's a place where there is nothing breakable within reach of the children. Everything is arranged with the young ones in mind.

On the other hand, when we visit other family, friends, or acquaintances whose children are already grown, married, or living away from home, their homes are filled with many fine, elegant, and costly items—most of which are almost always very fragile. At these places, we usually spend most of the visit running after the kids, telling them: "Don't touch that. No, don't go in there. Hey, get away from there right this minute. If you don't let go of that right now . . . ! Please let go of the cat before you smother it to death." This makes for a none-too-agreeable experience.

That's why when we visit "childproof" homes we feel as if we are in heaven. The adults can spend hours visiting without having to worry about someone breaking or getting into something they shouldn't.

They usually have plenty of toys and things to entertain the children.

We have very good, enjoyable conversations. We are very close friends and have many things in common. Our visits can last for hours. Sometimes three or four in the morning rolls around, and we are still "solving the world's problems." When we tell our kids that we are going to visit these friends, they get excited just at the prospect of it, and so do we.

That's the way it should be when we are expecting to have an encounter with God. We should be excited! A Christian who thinks he *has* to spend time with God, as if it were some dreaded obligation that must be "fulfilled" in order to continue being a Christian, has obviously lost his passion for the "house of the Lord." We should get excited just thinking about what a privilege it is to be in His presence.

Ahaz not only did not go to the sanctuary—he didn't even believe in it. He treated it contemptuously, offensively, and even robbed it of its beauty and utensils. On one occasion he took things from it in return for a favor he was expecting to receive from his supposed allies, which, by the way, did not bring about the desired results.

After closing down the Lord's house, Ahaz had another "wonderful" idea: "Let's set up altars everywhere," he said, "so that the people can worship their respective gods with greater ease and convenience." (See 2 Chronicles 28:24.) To me, this is yet another example of the fact that he was an undisciplined man. He had never been taught to go to the Lord's house, and now, knowing that there are many who did enter the temple for worship, he tries to come up with some kind of "convenient" plan to draw them out of the temple, too. He would take the altars closer to the people, out to the street, denigrating the one true God to the same position as all the gods of Baal that he had crafted. Can you see why he was such a wicked man? He had no concept of what it meant to worship the Lord.

The life of a true worshiper follows a discipline of "going" to the house of the Lord. It is absolutely necessary that we take the time and make the effort to seek the Lord's face. It is very important that we have the order and discipline to seek Him. This includes meeting with the local congregation in which the Lord has placed us. The writer of Hebrews states it so clearly:

> Let us not give up meeting together, as some are in the habit of doing, but let us encourage one another—and all the more as you see the Day approaching.
>
> —HEBREWS 10:25

It's true that the "house of the Lord" is not the place where we meet together every week—we ourselves are the temple. However, it is of utmost importance to come together with the other members of the body to be encouraged and to learn from one another. We must spend time together with the Lord, allowing God to speak in the corporate gathering, bringing direction, comfort, and meeting our needs.

There are those who would say, "We don't need to go to a service with everyone else. We meet right here in our home, and we find the Lord." I believe those people have lost sight of the main reason for the body meeting together: The Lord says He is building a spiritual dwelling place for God. (See Ephesians 2:19–22.) The meeting of the body together should be a joint expression of what we are experiencing individually. That is to say, just as we meet alone with the Lord in our homes, so it is important to get together with other members of the local body into which the Lord has placed us.

At the time that Hezekiah ascended the throne, the temple had been turned into a storehouse. One of the first things that Hezekiah did after taking the throne was to give the temple some much needed attention. Hezekiah reminds me of King David, one of his ancestors, who also felt that he could not rule without having the ark of the covenant with him.

When David became king of Israel, one of the first things he did was look for the ark of the presence of the Lord. (See 2 Samuel 6.) For many years under Saul's reign, the ark had been in the house of Abinadab in Kiriath Jearim. (See 1 Samuel 6:1–7:2.) Since Saul was not concerned with getting it back, there it stayed. David, however, knew that without the presence of the Lord in the midst of his people there was no protection, guidance, or direction. As a result, he gave himself to the task of returning the ark to the camp as soon as possible.

This shows us a little of the love David had for the presence of God, realizing that without the Lord, we are nothing and can do nothing.

Hezekiah also realized the importance of having God at the center of all of his activities, so he immediately repaired the Lord's house—it appears it was the first official business he set about to do.

GET BEYOND THE EXTERIOR

THE FIRST THING TO BE REPAIRED WAS THE FRONT DOOR—THAT which was exposed to the street, the superficial part of the temple, that which everyone could easily see. This represents an initial work. Upon coming to Christ, many people allow the Lord to deal with the obvious problems in their lives, those that stick out the most. As the Holy Spirit convicts them of sin, they begin to leave behind, one by one, those sins under which they've been living.

For example, the adulterer repents and begins living in fidelity. The drunkard stops drinking. The foul-mouthed curser stops using bad language. Those things that were easily detectable in the life of someone who previously had no awareness of God are now dropped. In that first "phase" we allow the Lord to give us a new paint job, fix us up a little here and there, dust us off, install a new lock and some new hinges, and *presto* . . . All exterior change—nothing else.

There is a very real danger for many newborn Christians in this initial phase. Learning how to do things without really knowing why they do them is comparable to repairing only the doors and not going inside to take care of the rest of our temple. If we don't teach newcomers how to develop a personal and intimate relationship with the Lord, most of them will settle for what they observe in others around them—merely a facade.

Many have learned more about our Christian subculture than about having a personal and intimate relationship with Jesus. For example, without even knowing it, we teach them a new way of talking. I say, "God bless you."

You answer, "Amen."

Or, as in some circles, I say, "The peace of Christ be with you."

You respond, "And with you, too."

We develop a whole set of rules and regulations that must be complied with in order to "belong." I've known people who have never been able to get past being "saved, sanctified, and filled with the Holy Ghost" as their personal testimony. If we were to ask them the definition of those three things, they probably wouldn't be able to give it. More than likely, it was a testimony they heard from someone else; it sounded good, so they adopted it for themselves.

In our efforts to help new believers "build the facade," we teach them how to dress, how to fix their hair, and a multitude of other things necessary to fit into our dearly protected Christian subculture. Soon, they are used to being told how to do things; they don't learn how to think for themselves. People are looking for leadership, and there is no shortage of those who give it to them.

I'm not belittling the need to be concerned with our external identity as a Christian. But in stressing the external, we fail to comprehend the reality of Jesus in our lives. All those "things" are really superficial. Telling people how to dress, walk, and talk will not help them to develop the ability to walk and talk on their own. But if we teach them to allow the Lord into the most intimate part of their lives, He will teach them *His* ways, and they will learn to walk in *His* paths (Ps. 25:4–5).

Let's not stop at the doors. Let's allow the Lord to complete the work that He has begun, and will perfect, in us (Phil. 1:6.)

When Hezekiah began to repair the temple, I can imagine people passing in front of the temple and saying, "Did you see? The temple has been repaired." From their vantage point on the street, it looked repaired. A peek inside would have revealed the destruction still within. The temple was still in ruins—even though the outside was beautiful. This is what the Lord refers to when He says, "Man looks at the outward appearance, but the LORD looks at the heart" (1 Sam. 16:7).

In spite of being raised in an ungodly home, Hezekiah understood the importance of the Lord's house. He declares:

> Our fathers were unfaithful; they did evil in the eyes of the LORD our God and forsook him. They turned their faces away from the LORD's dwelling place and turned their backs on him. They also shut the doors of the portico and put out the lamps. They did not

burn incense or present any burnt offerings at the sanctuary to the God of Israel. Therefore, the anger of the LORD has fallen ... he has made them an object of dread and horror and scorn, as you can see with your own eyes. This is why our fathers have fallen by the sword and why our sons and daughters and our wives are in captivity.

—2 CHRONICLES 29:6–9

Hezekiah understood what it meant to have a relationship with God. He mentioned the burning of incense, which represents prayer, praise, and worship (everything that goes up before God), as well as the offering of sacrifices and burnt offerings. He directly related the neglect of the temple with being enslaved, scorned, and made into an object of horror.

Isn't it true that someone who does not have a constant relationship with God finds himself enslaved? Haven't you noticed that when we no longer burn the incense of praise and worship, prayer and fasting, we begin to experience hindrances in our spiritual lives? Somehow Hezekiah understood that what was happening to the nation was directly related to the fact that they had abandoned God, and he decided to do something about it.

Note that after repairing the doors he spoke to the priests and Levites, the ministers of that day. He knew that the repairs needed to go much deeper than just fixing up the outside. There needed to be a major cleaning job on the inside.

I like the language the king uses in 2 Chronicles 29:10: "Now I intend to make a covenant with the LORD. . . . " He decided to do it. He gave this the importance it required. He wasn't going to let another day go by without getting this problem fixed. We often lack a determination to do things. We see indecision in the lives of many priests and Levites who minister today.

It's time to repair whatever is wrong in our lives.

Straighten it up, fix it, and give a thorough cleaning to our temples, so that the Lord's anger can be turned away (v. 10). Spiritual leaders need to be determined people. Locate the problem and take immediate and drastic measures to solve it, just as King Hezekiah did.

GOING "INTO"

THE KING'S WORDS MOVED THE PRIESTS, WHO CALLED A MEETING of all their brothers and made preparations for going into the Lord's house to clean it (v. 15). A small word in verse 16 catches my eye—it's the word *into*.

> The priests went *into* the sanctuary of the LORD to purify it. They brought out to the courtyard of the LORD's temple everything unclean that they found in the temple of the LORD . . . and carried it out.
>
> —EMPHASIS MINE

The word *into* implies that they went into the most remote corner of the temple. This brings us back to the heart. What are the things in our heart? What have we been "storing" there? Is there some area of our lives that we haven't completely given over to the Lord?

Nobody knows us better than we know ourselves, except for the Lord. We hide many things from other people, even from the people to whom we are the closest—including feelings, thoughts, desires, and attitudes. But it all is very clear to us and to God.

You don't have to tell the sinner that he is a sinner; he knows that very well. You don't have to reveal the carnality of many Christians because they know it very well (unless they are very deceived). But the truth of the matter is that we don't like to be told the truth about ourselves. We are experts at disguises, masks, and fronts in order to appear to be something that we are not.

A true worshiper needs to ask himself probing questions

that may hurt: *What is in my heart? What is my motivation for doing this? What areas of my life do I need to allow the Lord to cleanse?* I ask these questions frequently of myself. The answers may reveal our true condition— not the facade or the one we want everyone to believe.

What do you think about when you are alone? What thoughts do you have when everyone has gone home and you're no longer within the four comforting walls of your church or congregation? What are the things that go through your mind when you are alone in your bedroom after your family has gone to bed?

The answers to these and similar questions will give us a true reading of our heart's condition. We must allow the Lord to come "into" our temple and take out everything "unclean."

When Hezekiah's men cleaned out the temple, they took the unclean things into the courtyard and then outside the city. I can imagine that the people passing by couldn't believe all the stuff that had been stored inside. All that which was unclean was exposed to the public eye—right there in the temple courtyard! Not hidden from anyone! If the priests of Ahaz's day had taken out the trash daily, as they were supposed to do, all these unclean things would never have been exposed in the courtyard for all the world to see.

When we maintain our daily relationship with the Lord, not allowing the trash to accumulate, our uncleanness will not have to be exposed to the whole world. But when years go by without a cleansing work of God in our lives, there will come a time when everything will be exposed. The lesson is to allow the Lord to deal with us on a daily basis, daily allowing the Word to wash us (Eph. 5:26). Then we will not bring shame to the people of God or to the house of the Lord because of our sin and rebellion.

When Hezekiah called the priests and Levites to cleanse the temple, he first instructed them to "consecrate yourselves now" (2 Chron. 29:5). Leaders, pastors, evangelists, teachers, worship leaders, musicians, and all who are involved in the Lord's work must check our own motivations for service first. What kinds of things motivate us to be involved in the ministry? Are we in it because we want to be seen or noticed? Are we in it because we have a misguided desire to "lord" it over people? Could it be that our motivation is monetary gain from the ministry? Could it be a spirit of exhibitionism, where we want to shine the light on all of our talents and accomplishments? If the answer is *yes* to any of these questions, then there is an urgent need to go "into" our house for a major cleaning.

If we allow the Holy Spirit to cleanse our hearts thoroughly, our uncleanness won't be exposed some sad day for all the world to see. Make a list of all the questions that will lead to a revelation of your true motives. Don't stray from the true purpose for ministry.

Listen to the questions posed by people who love you—your spouse, pastors, and leaders. These people have invested time, tears, advice, and support into your ministry. Have someone to whom you can listen and from whom you can receive advice and direction. Through them you may discover something hidden in your heart that you had never known was there.

When we are expecting guests in our home, we make everything ready to receive them in the way in which they deserve to be received. On occasion, with embarrassment, we say, "Please excuse the mess," when someone "drops in" unexpectedly. Or we close the door to certain rooms that are still messy. We do everything possible to keep our guests from going into that particular room.

In the same way, many times we have told the Lord, "Take control of my life. I give You the keys to all the areas of my heart," but behind His back we hide that little key that opens the door to the room that is in disarray. The Lord, taking us at our word, begins to inspect all the areas. We say to Him, "Lord, here's the living room."

He says, "I would like to go into that room."

"Lord, look at this other bedroom," we answer Him. "It has a king-sized bed, carpet, and all the conveniences You could ever imagine. Stay here, Lord."

But He insists, "I would really like to see *that* room."

"But, Lord," we answer, "aren't You interested in seeing my beautiful new kitchen with mahogany cabinets and a top-of-the-line stove and microwave?"

Still the Lord answers, "I want to go into that place."

No matter how much we protest, we can't hide anything from the Lord. Finally He says, "What about that key you are holding in your hand? What are we going to do about that one?"

It's time to give up and allow Him to enter that disorderly room—it will be worth it. He will not only help us to clean it out, He will also give us the strength ("grace") to keep it clean the rest of our lives. We must give Christ the keys "into" all the areas of our lives so that His purifying work can keep us in optimum condition to serve Him and His body.

Hezekiah's men put a lot of time and energy into cleaning the house: "They began . . . on the first day of the first month . . . finishing on the sixteenth day of the first month" (29:17). Sixteen days! It wasn't an overnight job; it took some time. When we have fallen into uncleanness, it is true that the grace of God will pick us up. But the fact that His grace is sufficient shouldn't give us the attitude that restoration is some sort of simplified automatic process. There should be true repentance in our lives—not just a "Band-Aid" prayer of five minutes and that's the end of it. We need to go before the Lord with "a broken and contrite heart" (Ps. 51:17). Take the time necessary to allow Him to pull out the roots of uncleanness that have controlled us for so long. Unless we give Him the chance to deal with the root of the problem, we only "pull up" the surface, and that same sin can spring up in our lives again in the not-so-distant future. When it comes to your heart, allow the Lord to "guard" it continually (Prov. 4:23).

WE'RE DONE...AREN'T WE?

THE PRIESTS CAME TO HEZEKIAH TO INFORM HIM THAT THEY were finished cleaning the house and all the utensils used in worship. They probably expected the king to congratulate them and thank them for a wonderful job well done.

But no. Instead of that, Hezekiah knew something that we've been trying to learn throughout this entire chapter: There is a matter at hand much deeper than just cleaning out the temple. The answers must be found to some important questions: Why did the people begin to use the Lord's house as a storehouse? Why was it so easy for them to desecrate the Lord's dwelling place?

The king understood that the answers to these questions would be found in the people's hearts. Their hearts had grown far from God. Now was not the time for celebrating—at least not yet. The time had come for *repentance*—asking forgiveness for falling to such deep levels of sin and spiritual negligence.

This king's courage is admirable. His commitment to doing things correctly is a wonderful trait. He wasn't in a hurry to celebrate before repairing the damage that had been done. He is to be admired for guiding the entire nation in the process of repentance. Many leaders want other people to do the dirty work, instead of taking the reins themselves and being the first to recognize their error, sin, and separation from God.

Some have the mistaken idea that as leaders we shouldn't allow our people to see us humbled because we may lose our authority. But look at the example of Jesus—He humbled Himself even to the cross, taking on the form of a servant (Phil. 2:5–8). Hezekiah knew that unless his nation saw him responding to the conviction of God with repentance, it would be difficult for them to humble themselves.

In verse 21 of 2 Chronicles 29, as the people brought their sin offerings to the altar, the nation of Israel cried out in repentance: "We have sinned; we need God's forgiveness."

Hezekiah knew the importance of admitting that the decadence of Israel was not simply a consequence of the passage of time—but a voluntary act of estrangement from God—and this required repentance. To keep our house clean, we need to live a life of constant repentance before the Lord, not taking things for granted, but recognizing that we serve a great God, fearful, jealous, and just. He is always seeking for a people who understand that they must walk before Him in justice and righteousness.

After the sin offering was burned, the sacrificial animal was unrecognizable—only the ashes remained. The only things left on the altar were the ashes of something that had been but no longer was. In the same way, we should live our lives upon the altar in a constant state of repentance, allowing the consuming fire of God to burn all the straw, leaves, and rubbish in our lives until there is nothing left. We must lose our identity (in the carnal sense) and allow the identity of Christ to shine in our lives. Our lives should look like fine ashes, without character or identity except for Christ's. This can only happen as we allow the Lord to put us upon the altar.

As a young man I used to sing a song called "Send the Fire." Although we sang it with sincerity, the focus of that song was wrong. It was one of the many self-centered songs that we sang, always asking the Lord for something: "Send the fire . . . " "We want revival . . " "Give me this . . . " "Give me that..."

One night after I had led the worship in our little church in a small town close to where we lived, my mother asked me, "Why do you always sing that song 'Send the Fire'?"

"Well, because the young people like it," I answered her.

"Do you know that the Lord's fire burns?" she asked. "It's true that it represents revival, but remember that for revival to come, the Lord has to burn all the sin that is in our lives. So if you're going to sing that song, do it with the understanding that you're asking the Lord to burn you, *and don't be surprised if He does.*"

I have never forgotten her words, and from that day forward I have rarely sung that song again.

NOW . . . LET'S PARTY!

WHEN ALL OF THE REPAIR WORK HAD BEEN COMPLETED AND ALL of the nation had been led into repentance, the people entered into celebration, and the music began. When I read this passage before, I had only read the part about the music and praise beginning—never understanding that it was a result of everything that had happened earlier. It is impossible to freely enter into praise and worship without first having a real encounter with God.

Hezekiah continued to be a worship leader. He bowed down before the Lord and commanded the Levites to play their instruments. Now the atmosphere is changed—charged with the intensity of the people's rejoicing, joy, happiness, celebration, and worship. The last verse of this chapter says, "Hezekiah and all the people rejoiced" (2 Chron. 29:36). After God has done everything that needs to be done in our hearts, we can enter into the festivity with all our being.

When the heart is right, when we have entered "into" forgiveness, the stage is set for a true celebration. Such a celebration cannot be faked—it is something that comes from a man or woman who is clean, pure, and justified within, who has taken the time to humble himself or herself before God so He can fix the heart.

Once I understood this chapter in the Bible, I realized

that worship is the result of having had an encounter with God. It is an outward expression of an inner work.

Don't allow pride, understanding, experience, or anything else to keep you from humbling yourself before God. We need Him more and more every day. Allow His burning and purifying fire to cleanse you from all the things that create "uncleanness" inside your temple. Guard your heart so that you will become a true worshiper.

God does not want robots,
but men and women
who gladly, desirously, lovingly,
and committedly choose
to have a relationship with Him.

Four

Worship

WORSHIP AS A LIFESTYLE COMES AT A VERY HIGH PRICE; FEW men and women are willing to pay the price. For many, praise is not as difficult; most of us have the innate desire to celebrate. We all enjoy a good party! Especially those of us from a Latin culture and society.

I once boarded a plane in Bombay, India, where some people on board could be heard talking in loud, happy voices from all the way in the back of the plane. I wasn't surprised to find out that it was a group of happy Latinos, Puerto Ricans to be exact, on their way back home. It didn't take us more than thirty minutes to know their names, their personal history, the names of their children, and any other detail of interest to us. We Latins have an atmosphere about us. We are a warm, hospitable, dynamic, and enthusiastic people. We love to party, celebrate, and have a good time!

All of these are great characteristics for praise, but they

don't help us to discipline ourselves in worship. In Latin America it is never uncommon to have the neighbors throw a very loud all-night party with lots of people in attendance. Before the night is over, they've played hundreds of songs that can be heard all over the neighborhood. Many times a live mariachi band will participate in the festivities. My wife and I have lain in bed many times, kept awake by the loud music and laughter from a party. We don't even have to have a really good reason to throw a party.

In John 4, Jesus meets a Samaritan woman. During the entire conversation, He talks to her about the subject of worship. At first, she tries to steer the conversation away from that to talk about racial differences. However, Jesus is not distracted; He speaks to her about living water. Thinking that He is speaking about natural water, she tells Him to give her some of that water so she would not have to come draw water from the well anymore.

Jesus stays focused on worship. Then the woman begins to speak about the origin of the well and who drinks from it, but Jesus continues speaking about worship. When the Lord confronts her about her husbands, she tries to distract Him with questions about religion and prophecy. But Jesus comes right back to the essence of what He's been trying to tell her from the very beginning: She needs to learn about worship.

This scene is so typical of people today. If you try to deal with them concerning their relationship with God, some will try to talk about racial problems. Others, particularly Latin Americans, want to discuss "the tradition and religion our parents taught us." Some try to tell you about their physical needs and lacks, while others will argue about biblical prophecy or different doctrines and denominations. Yet Jesus keeps coming back to the same topic: "The Father is seeking true worshipers." Jesus gets to the point. He wants to know one thing: Are you going to be a true worshiper or are you going to be like the

Samaritans who "worship what you do not know"? (John 4:22).

> Yet a time is coming and has now come when the true worshipers will worship the Father in spirit and truth, for they are the kind of worshipers the Father seeks. God is spirit, and his worshipers must worship in spirit and in truth.
>
> —JOHN 4:23–24

TRUE WORSHIPERS

IT SHOULD CATCH OUR ATTENTION THAT THE FATHER IS NOT SEEKING "praisers." There are many praisers all over the place. Praise, because it's festive and happy by nature, tends to draw people quickly. Praise doesn't carry the same commitment that worship does, as we will see later on. The Father seeks, needs, desires, and yearns for worshipers.

It is equally important to note that He does not seek "worship" but "worshipers"—people who are committed, submitted, and dedicated to rendering worship to Him. God created us to have communion with Him. He wants a relationship with someone who has the free will to desire to be with Him. He has never forced anyone to be with Him, and He never will. The Father desires that we make the decision to be with Him because that is what *we* want. Every man and woman has a basic desire for someone who wants to be with him or her. But forcing a relationship makes the situation very uncomfortable for all parties involved.

I've had the privilege many times of sharing the gospel at some concert, breakfast, dinner, or other kind of event that was organized to bring people to Christ. At almost every one of these events there are certain number of people in attendance under duress. More than likely, they did not choose to be there, but happened to get there because of someone's insistence. These people are easily recognizable—their faces are twisted into a frown, their arms crossed as they try to communicate their complete disinterest in being there. They are hoping that the person who brought them will notice their complete unhappiness and never invite them again.

I've watched mothers who have coerced children to come who would much rather be with friends or someplace else. The mother, smiling ear to ear, turns to look at her offspring every few minutes to encourage him or her to enjoy the program as much as she is. Meanwhile, the child tries to show his or her unwillingness to be there so that the mother will get tired and leave him or her alone.

We know that God wants us to want to be with Him. If it were not this way, He could have programmed us to do certain things at certain times like robots. One robot could be programmed to pray, meditate, praise, go to church (on time), not gossip, not hurt anyone, read the Word, share the gospel, pay the tithes and offerings (without complaining), and thousands of other things every day. This seems like it could have been a good alternative for the Lord. He could have had perfect Christians by just programming their computers.

But He didn't want it that way, and He still doesn't. He desires to have an intimate, direct, and voluntary personal relationship with each of us. God does not want robots, but men and women who gladly, desirously, lovingly, and committedly choose to have a relationship with Him.

This is not a difficult concept for someone in love to understand. We seek out our beloved. We hope for moments alone together to see each other, talk, hold hands, go for a walk, and all those wonderfully romantic things that people do when they're in love. A relationship doesn't just happen overnight—it takes years to grow. As it is cultivated, it rises to new levels of confidence and commitment, until it reaches the highest level of commitment—marriage.

Our relationship with the Father should be the same.

He is not seeking "worship"; He is seeking you—the worshiper.

Your worship will be limited by your knowledge of God. You will not be capable of worshiping Him beyond your knowledge of Him. If you don't know that He is faithful, how will you be able to say, "Lord, You are faithful"? Unless you have proven His mercy, you won't be able to say with assurance, "I praise You because You are merciful."

It is so vital to develop an intimate, loving, fresh relationship with Him. We must know Him for ourselves—not because someone told us about Him, or because we read of Him somewhere. He is seeking people who will develop a close relationship with Him.

Notice that He is not seeking just any kind of worshiper, but a true worshiper. The world today is filled with deception. People disguise themselves as many different things in order to take advantage of something or someone. Today, more than ever, we need the gift of "discerning of spirits." (See 1 Corinthians 12:10, NKJV.)

To be the kind of worshiper that the Father is looking for, we're going to have to take off the masks and be genuine with God.

One of the most popular and effective masks with which Satan has deceived many is the mask of religiosity. Many hide the reality of who they are behind this mask. It gives a semblance of outward piousness or holiness so that everyone will admire how dedicated we are to God.

A person wearing the mask of a religious spirit will follow the rules—dot the i's and cross the t's. Life will be a series of *dos* and *don'ts*.

Jesus said the Father is seeking "true worshipers." Many of us are *sincere,* but not *true* worshipers. All over the world every Sunday, millions of this kind of worshiper congregate. They sing the songs and go through the motions—they may even be sincere in congregating—but their heart is far from God. The Lord wants more than just the motions; He wants our heart. He is looking for a *true* worshiper, not just a sincere one.

> The Lord says: "These people come near to me with their mouth and honor me with their lips, but their hearts are far from me. Their worship of me is made up only of rules taught by men."
>
> —ISAIAH 29:13

SPIRIT AND TRUTH

"SPIRIT AND TRUTH" IS PROBABLY ONE OF THE MOST-USED PHRASES in many Christian circles. Some have used it to excuse their disorderly and unbridled way of worshiping God. To others it is a popular catch phrase of the Christian subculture. For example, before singing a song a worship leader may say, "Sing this as unto the Lord. Do it with all your heart, because the Bible says we are to worship Him *in spirit and in truth.*" The leader may say the words so quickly that they have no effect on the hearts of the listeners.

SPIRIT

JOHN 4:24 TELLS US THAT "GOD IS SPIRIT, AND HIS WORSHIPERS must worship in spirit and in truth." This verse establishes that true worship is communion of our spirit with God's Spirit. The desire to worship God is born in the very depths of man (his spirit). It's important to remember that we *are spirit,* we *have a soul,* and we *live in this flesh called the body.* Most of us don't have this progression clearly in mind, and we live more for the flesh than for the spirit. But in the end, what will stand before the throne of God to give account for our actions, words, and thoughts will not be our flesh but our spirit.

Our spirit controls our worship of God, not our flesh or our soul. Jesus did not say, "In flesh and in truth"; nor did He say, "In soul and in truth." He said, "In spirit and in truth."

King David settled this issue in his life at an early age. While he was out with his sheep he began writing the most incredible hymnal of all time—the Psalms. We can see the psalmist's character and personality through these powerful writings. Sometimes it was sweet and tender. (See Psalm 23.) At other times it was tempestuous, even violent. (See Psalm 149.) On other occasions he broaches subjects such as personal needs and internal and emotional struggles. (See Psalms 7 and 13.)

But what comes to my mind as I read David's psalms is the fact that he was a man of discipline and determination. He resolved to do things—and he did them. He didn't allow his emotions or feelings to dictate his worship of God. Time after time we see how he resolved to worship God; he understood that worship has to come from man's spirit and not from his soul or his body. Let's look at David's psalms:

> I will praise you, O LORD, with all my heart;
>> I will tell of all your wonders.
> I will be glad and rejoice in you;
>> I will sing praise to your name, O Most High.
>> —PSALM 9:1–2

> I call to the LORD, who is worthy of praise,
>> and I am saved from my enemies.
>> —PSALM 18:3

> I will extol the LORD at all times;
>> his praise will always be on my lips.
>> —PSALM 34:1

> My heart is steadfast, O God;
>> I will sing and make music with all my soul.
> Awake, harp and lyre!
>> I will awaken the dawn.
> I will praise you, O LORD, among the nations;

I will sing of you among the peoples.

—PSALM 108:1–3

Praise the LORD.
I will extol the LORD with all my heart
   in the council of the upright and in the assembly.

—PSALM 111:1

I will praise you, O LORD, with all my heart;
   before the "gods" I will sing your praise.
I will bow down toward your holy temple
   and will praise your name
   for your love and your faithfulness,
for you have exalted above all things
   your name and your word.

—PSALM 138:1–2

I will exalt you, my God the King;
   I will praise your name for ever and ever.
Every day I will praise you
   and extol your name for ever and ever.

—PSALM 145:1–2

Each one of these verses demonstrates an act of resolve on David's part. He didn't write, "If everything goes well, then I will praise You." "If my boss doesn't yell at me, I will bless You." "If my wife wakes up in a good mood and doesn't burn the toast, I will exalt You." "If I can have that new car I've been asking You for, I will glorify You."

But people do say these things. Some even go so far as to say, "What's more, You won't hear anything else out of me until You give me that new car." It sounds incredible, but there are persons who act that way with God. They think praise is negotiable for things they want from God, such as His favor, mercy, and blessing. God, have mercy on us!

Worship was something David resolved to do in his heart because he understood that his spirit was in control of the worship in his life—not his soul (emotions) or his body. The moment we realize this, we will step closer to becoming a true worshiper.

Some protest: "But that was *David;* I am not David, and I don't have his faith—or the favor he had with God." David wasn't special. He was just a common man. When God told the prophet Samuel to anoint one of Jesse's sons to be the next king of Israel, David wasn't even invited! (See 1 Samuel 16.) Samuel made the rounds among David's brothers, supposing one of them would be a good king because of their physical attributes or abilities.

When God didn't choose any of them, Samuel was so sure God had told him the new king would come from Jesse's house that he was willing to go out on a limb by asking, "Could there be another son that isn't here?"

Jesse halfheartedly replied, "There is still the youngest . . . but he is tending the sheep" (v. 11). To everyone's surprise, Samuel called for David.

I can imagine this first appearance of David. Without knowing what was going on, David came in with his little harp in hand and wearing his hand-me-down clothes. Maybe his clothes were even patched, mended, and ill-fitting, and more than likely they smelled like sheep. He had no opportunity to go take a bath and change his clothes as his brothers had probably done.

I can almost see his older brothers' faces when David walked into the house: "Hmmm, *he's* here." Imagine what they must have thought when the prophet took the horn and poured the oil over David's head, anointing him to the position of king—"in the presence of his brothers" (1 Sam. 16:1–13).

What did the Lord tell Samuel He was looking at? *The heart* (v. 7). David did not have a greater aptitude than his brothers. What's more, it is very likely that he may have had less abilities than they had. God did not choose his brothers, however, because they did not have David's heart: willing, ready, surrendered, and determined to seek God at all times. We are the Davids of today; we can determine to worship God in our hearts, and we can discipline ourselves to do it.

If you don't feel that you have the qualifications for being a "true worshiper," then you are an excellent candidate. God can use you:

> But God chose the foolish things of the world to shame the wise; God chose the weak things of the world to shame the strong. He chose the lowly things of this world and the despised things—and the things that are not—to nullify the things that are, so that no one may boast before him.
> —1 CORINTHIANS 1:27–29

The Spirit of God dwells in our spirit; that's why it is important to allow the spirit to direct the worship in our lives—God's Spirit is in direct communion with God. One psalm describes it like this: "Deep calls to deep in the roar of your waterfalls" (Ps. 42:7). The word *deep* refers to a place of profound depth. From the depth of our being (our spirit) we call to the depth of God's being (His Spirit) to have communion. The roar of waterfalls is symbolic of all the noises, sounds, problems, and circumstances that surround us in this life. In spite of the roar of those waterfalls, our spirit desires to have more communion with God's Spirit.

Christ said, "The spirit is willing, but the body is weak" (Matt. 26:41). The original word for *willing* is *prothumos,* which means "ready." The word for *weak* in the original is *asthenes,* which means "impotent, sickly, without power." This is yet another lesson from Jesus' own mouth about the need to give the spirit more power, and the flesh less of it, to direct the affairs of our life. The spirit is *ready* for communion with God, but the flesh is impotent and powerless to commune with God.

TRUTH

GOD ALSO INSTRUCTS US TO WORSHIP HIM IN *TRUTH*. JESUS IS teaching the importance of using our understanding when we worship. The apostle Paul talked to the Corinthians about the role of understanding in worship in 1 Corinthians 14:15: "I will pray with my spirit, but I will also pray with my mind; I will sing with my spirit, but I will also sing with my mind."

Many people want some extraordinary "something" to come over them and "take" them to a place of worship without any effort on their part. However, true worship involves action on the part of the worshiper. We must worship Him on the basis of our understanding of the truths about Him. This makes our worship in spirit and "truth" based on the "truths" of *who* He is.

Our understanding of the truths of who He is comes from knowing the truths and principles declared in His Word about who He is. Our worship, to be worship in truth, must be based on *the truth* of His Word. Unless a "new" way or method to worship the Lord is compatible with the everlasting Word of truth, then it simply is not acceptable. Our worship must be based solidly in the Word of God.

Years ago a teacher told me something that impressed me greatly. He said, "All of the revelations of God have already been received. The only thing that can be said today is that God is illuminating us about His revelations."

He was speaking about the Bible, of course. It is the revealed Word of God, perfect and infallible. Many of us say, "God revealed this or that to me." To state it more accurately, we should say, "God enlightened me about this or that concerning His revelation." To be able to worship in "truth" we need to know His Word, the Bible.

The word *truth* also refers to worshiping the Lord with

65

sincerity, integrity, and purity of heart. For many years it was believed that the only thing you needed to be able to worship was a sincere heart. Although sincerity of heart is very important in worship, sincerity in itself is not what worship is all about.

Year after year we see rituals and ceremonies being held in countries around the world to commemorate some deity or idol. Without a doubt, these people worship their gods with great sincerity. Their processions and celebrations are planned with great care, because they sincerely want to please their gods. Yet, does the simple fact that they are sincere justify the fact that they are committing acts of what the Bible clearly sets down as idolatry?

Are we going to say then that if we are sincere in our worship we can go on living in all types of error? Of course not. As we come to know more of His nature and character, we come face to face with our need to change our way of worship in accordance with His truth and not according to our own.

The word *sincerity* has a very interesting root. To be a *sincere* person means to be someone "without a mask." In ancient times, they made wax masks to wear to the great masked balls given by the kings. To be sincere came to mean "without wax." When deals were made in the business world, the individuals involved would ask each other, "Are you sincere?" In other words, "Are you hiding something behind a mask of wax? Have you taken off your mask so that I can see you entirely?" With this question they were able to determine if the person with whom they were dealing was unmasked.

In effect, to be a true worshiper, it is necessary to take off the masks that hide our true selves so that we can worship the Lord sincerely. Although sincerity is not the only ingredient for being a true worshiper, it is one of the most necessary. When we draw near to God, it should be with a pure, honest, and maskless heart. The "truth" of our life should come to light when we are in His presence.

Another aspect of worshiping in "truth" is worshiping *by* the truth: Jesus. On one occasion He said, "I am . . . the truth" (John 14:6). We have to learn to worship through Jesus Christ, since He is the truth. In Colossians 3:17 we read: "And whatever you do, whether in word or deed, do it all in the name of the Lord Jesus, giving thanks to God the Father through him." The Book of Hebrews teaches us that Jesus is our High Priest (Heb. 8:1–6). He "sat down at the right hand of the throne of the Majesty in heaven, and . . . serves in the sanctuary" (vv. 1–2). Our worship has to be given through our high priest, Jesus Christ. In 1 Timothy 2:5 Paul says, "For there is one God and one mediator between God and men, the man Christ Jesus."

SEEKS

JOHN 4:23 TELLS US THAT THE FATHER IS *SEEKING* FOR TRUE worshipers. It is sad to think that the God of the universe, the creator of heaven and earth, has to *seek* worshipers. After all, this is what we were created for. God wanted communion, relationship, and friendship with us, yet He still has to seek those who want to develop this relationship with Him. How sad!

Consider the following passages that reveal the Father's desire for communion with His people:

> . . . the people I formed for myself that they may proclaim my praise.
>
> —ISAIAH 43:21

> He predestined us to be adopted as his sons through Jesus Christ . . . to the praise of his glorious grace.
>
> —EPHESIANS 1:5–6

> For by him all things were created . . . all things were created by him and for him.
>
> —COLOSSIANS 1:16

The Bible repeatedly compares our relationship with the Lord to the marriage bond. His church (you and I) are the Lamb's (Jesus') bride, and one great day we will be united to Him in marriage for all eternity.

Yet we still have not learned to respond to our Bridegroom as we ought. Let's take a look at how the bride often conducts herself.

The Beloved comes and says, "Will you give Me a hug?"

And the bride (us) responds, "After I finish washing Your children's clothes and making your children's meals, Lord."

Once again the Beloved comes to us and asks, "Now, will you give Me a hug?"

And the bride answers, "As soon as I finish planning these programs and attending these meetings, Lord."

The bride is busy washing, ironing, cooking, changing, rocking, feeding the children, and talking to the neighbors (evangelization) about the wonderful Husband she has. Or the bride is busy working long hours to build a strong financial base, scheduling important meetings, meeting deadlines, building a business, and preparing programs for a local body of believers. The bride doesn't have time to be with the Bridegroom. When the day ends, she is so tired that she throws herself into bed to regain strength. The next day she continues with the same routine, beginning the morning with a hurried prayer: "Bless my day and my schedule, and please, try to understand that since I'm so busy in Your work, I won't have time to be with You today."

Rarely does the bride take the time to ask, "What is Your schedule for me today, Lord?"

The desire to have communion with us is in God's heart, but we deny Him that communion. Maybe we deny it for lack of understanding about God and what His desires are. Or maybe it is because we are so busy doing things *for* Him that we don't take time to simply be *with* Him. Many in full-time ministry tend to become so busy with things, all of them probably good, that we don't have any time left to spend with our Beloved. We have become so preoccupied with the work of the Lord that we have forgotten the Lord of the work.

I can't seem to put out of my mind the picture of a tender, loving God, One who is longing for friendship and communion with His beloved—the image of a loving Bridegroom walking the earth, searching, calling, speaking to the bride's heart in hope of slowing her down long enough to give Him the hug He desires. Will He find someone willing to stop long enough to have fellowship with Him?

*F*ew are willing
to get off the throne of their own lives
and allow the King of the universe
to sit there, to govern all their activities,
thoughts, and words.

Five

Why Is There a Shortage of True Worshipers?

WORSHIP IS NOT SOMETHING THAT COMES NATURALLY TO many people. In this chapter, I would like to look at some of the reasons and see if there are any solutions to the problem of a shortage of true worshipers. However, if you are not willing to become a true worshiper, I advise you to close this book quickly; what you read will challenge you to become committed to living according to what the Lord will reveal to you.

Everything has a price. This is a fact . . . a reality. Usually, the bigger the object or responsibility, the higher the price for it. There are some who believe and teach that everything that has to do with the gospel is easy—so they tend to oversimplify it. Others make the gospel difficult and unattainable with all kinds of rules and conditions about anything having to do with serving Christ. Without going to either one of these extremes, we have to touch on one point: Worship has a price—and

71

sometimes it is a high one.

THE PRICE FOR BOWING

IN JOHN 4:23, JESUS TELLS THE SAMARITAN WOMAN, "YET A TIME is coming and has now come when the true worshipers will worship the Father in spirit and truth, for they are the kind of worshipers the Father seeks."

The word used for "worshipers" by Jesus is *proskunetes,* meaning "someone who practices worship (*proskuneo*)."

Proskuneo (worship) means "to fall upon the knees and touch the ground with the forehead as an expression of profound reverence; kneeling or prostration to do homage or make obeisance." This is the type of worshipers of which there needs to be more: those who prostrate themselves before the throne of God in reverence, humility, and recognition of Him as the King of kings and Lord of lords. This is why there are so few worshipers. Few people want to pay the price of prostration; it would mean losing control of their lives, and many don't want to be out of control of their lives.

If we read John 4:23 in light of the word Jesus used, it takes on a whole new meaning. It would then read like this: "True prostrators prostrate themselves before the Father in spirit and in truth, for they are the kind of prostrators the Father seeks."

One of worship's main functions is to show us *our* position before the Lord. It isn't necessary to remind the Lord that He is seated on the throne of power, authority, and dominion. He already knows that. It is absolutely necessary to remind ourselves that He is the ultimate authority. This is something we do through worship.

Through the prophet Isaiah, the Lord says: "As the heavens are higher than the earth, so are my ways higher than your ways and my thoughts than your thoughts" (Isa. 55:9). This is a truth that we should always remember; it is important that it seep into the very fiber of who we are. We need to live and breathe this truth constantly: "He is higher in every way than I am." Worship allows us to maintain our focus on this eternal truth: "Lord, You are everything. In You I move, breathe, and have my being. Outside of You I never was and never would be anything." (See Acts 17:28.)

As we bow before His throne we are prostrating ourselves before Someone much bigger and more powerful than ourselves, thereby showing humility and surrender, signifying the recognition of our own weakness before our all-powerful Master.

In Revelation 4, the twenty-four elders bow before the throne, and as they bow, they do something unforgettable: "They lay their crowns before the throne" (v. 10). How significant! *A crown represents royalty*—kings wear crowns. It is the symbol for someone of importance, someone separated and distinguished. The various crowns in royal families symbolize different positions within the royal hierarchy, just as there are specific crowns that are used only on specified occasions or holidays. Crowns are a very important part of royalty.

Crowns are also used as prizes for the winners of sporting activities. On several occasions, Paul uses sports to illustrate biblical truths he is teaching in his epistles, mentioning crowns that are given as a reward. (See 1 Corinthians 9:24–26; 2 Timothy 2:5.) The Bible speaks of a crown as the reward for our faithfulness (2 Tim. 4:8; James 1:12; Rev. 2:10). Crowns are rewards that bring glory (recognition).

The twenty-four elders of Revelation wore crowns. Perhaps they are members of royalty or some of the ones who "won the race" and thus received crowns. Regardless of how they obtained their crowns, it is important to note that they recognize that their glory, however great, can't compare with the glory of the King of eternity. Upon seeing Him seated upon the throne, their immediate, almost natural, reaction is to "lay their crowns [that

73

which gives them glory and distinction] before the throne." Whatever glory or honor they may have is worthy only to be stepped on by the King of heaven, who has, in truth, the greatest and most excellent glory of all.

Perspective Worship gives us the opportunity to remember and affirm, "He is ALL; I am nothing. His ways are higher than my ways. His thoughts are higher than my thoughts." You and I need to worship, for by so doing we remember these truths and principles. If we don't worship, we will quickly forget our position of surrender at His feet, laying our crowns before His throne of justice, truth, and eternal glory.

Paul writes to the Philippians:

> But whatever was to my profit I now consider loss for the sake of Christ. What is more, I consider everything a loss compared to the surpassing greatness of knowing Christ Jesus my Lord, for whose sake I have lost all things. I consider them rubbish, that I may gain Christ....
>
> —PHILIPPIANS 3:7–8

The true worshiper recognizes the need to live a life of prostration before the throne of God in acknowledgment of the greatness of the King of kings and Lord of lords. The *New Bible Dictionary* says this about a throne: "A throne symbolizes dignity and authority (Gen. 41:40; 2 Sam. 3:10), which may extend beyond the immediate occupant (2 Sam. 7:13–16)...Righteousness and justice are therefore enjoined upon its occupants (Prov. 16:12; 20:28)."[1]

Yet there is another throne upon which many believers are firmly ensconced, with no chance of anyone else occupying that place of authority. That throne is the throne of our lives. This is one of the reasons why there are few true worshipers. Few are willing to get off the throne of their own lives and allow the King of the universe to sit there, to govern all their activities, thoughts, and words.

Oh, we're good at honoring the Lord with our lips and singing many beautiful songs about allowing the Lord to come and sit on the throne of our lives, but in practice and in reality, it isn't true. We have not bothered to get down off the throne of our lives and give that place to the One who should occupy it: Jesus Christ, King of kings.

Psalm 22:3 says, "But thou art holy, O thou that inhabitest the praises of Israel" (KJV). The word *inhabitest* in Hebrew is *yashab,* and it means "to sit, dwell, remain, have one's abode." One of the definitions for the word *sit* is "to be set." This is very significant; when we worship the Lord by singing to Him, bowing before Him figuratively or literally, we are creating a place where He can descend and stay with us. We are making a place for Him to sit down—a throne.

Once He's on the throne, He can do all the things a king does while sitting on the throne—reign, issue edicts, treat people favorably, judge, and exercise authority.

There is another understanding of the word *proskuneo* (worship) that I found very interesting. It is a compound of two Greek words: *pros,* which means "forward" (referring to direction) and *kuon,* which means "a dog, a hound" (literal or figurative). From these two words we get one of the meanings of *proskuneo,* "to kiss, as a dog kisses the hand of its master." This took me by surprise! I never imagined that worship had anything to do with dogs. But as I thought about that meaning one afternoon, I suddenly understood the reason for comparing worship to a dog's kissing the hand of its master.

There are many types of kisses today. There are social kisses, according to each country's culture. In Argentina men kiss each other on the cheek, something not done in Mexico (and we hope to goodness it stays that way). In many European countries, men greet each other with not one kiss but two—one on each cheek! There are family kisses: children kissing parents, parents kissing children, husbands kissing wives, and so on. Many times a kiss is given with the expectancy of receiving something in return, or it is given to make a good impression or as a sign of respect for a certain person. At other times, a kiss is a sign of betrayal, as when Judas betrayed Jesus.

It is interesting that the kind of kiss used in defining *proskuneo* is the kind a little dog gives its master. Many of us have been the owner of a puppy. There are some owners who go overboard in the care of their pet, spending a lot of money because they love their pets. There are others who abuse their pets, not feeding their pets for days and never paying any attention to them except to kick them and yell at them.

Yet in both extremes just described, the dog is loyal and devoted to its owner. Whether loved or abused, a puppy will greet its owner with licks on the hands and face. Why? The animal will always receive its owner in such a way until the day it dies, simply because of *who* his master is. That's it in a nut shell. That dog loves him simply because he recognizes him as his master.

The same should be true of our worship to God. This is what makes that aspect of the definition of the word *proskuneo* significant: Our praise of Him should not be based on what He does or doesn't do for us, but should be based on the reality that *He is who He is*. He is God! He is sovereign, majestic, marvelous, eternal, divine, just, true, and faithful. We worship Him because He is our God.

If He never gave us another thing, if we never received another blessing from His hand, He would still be *worthy* to receive glory and praise because of *who He is*.

THE PRICE FOR APPROACHING THE THRONE

ANOTHER REASON FOR THE SHORTAGE OF TRUE WORSHIPERS IS THE fact that entering the presence of God carries with it a big responsibility—one that many are not willing to accept, preferring to remain in the "courts" or at the "gates." The psalmist writes in Psalm 100: "Enter his gates with thanksgiving and his courts with praise" (v. 4). This is a reference to the physical structure of Moses' tabernacle, establishing for us today a protocol for entering the presence of God. Let's study this for a few minutes.

The vast majority of Israelites in Bible days never had any contact with God beyond the gates and courts of the tabernacle or temple. The holy place was reserved for only a few of the priests, and an even smaller number of priests were ever allowed to enter the holy of holies. Only one man could enter the holy of holies on one day of the year (the Day of Atonement). It was there in the holy of holies where the very presence of God dwelt.

The common people knew about the holy of holies only by what was told them by the priests, who were told about it by other priests. I can imagine that there existed a great chain of misinformation. It's possible that very interesting stories circulated about the holy of holies, some based, for example, on the experience of the story told to the cousin of the brother-in-law of the priest who was in charge of cleaning the tabernacle. The only thing everyone knew without a doubt was that the presence of the Lord of Hosts was awesome and fearsome, something to be greatly respected.

When Moses was on Mount Sinai with God, the whole nation could hear the thunder and see the lightning; they knew that Jehovah God was Someone great and powerful. I suppose the great majority of the Israelites were happy that they didn't have to deal directly with God. I can just picture them coming near to the tabernacle with fear and trembling, hoping they hadn't done something that would get them into trouble.

The Bible tells us that the high priest wore special robes on the day he entered into the holy of holies. Sewn into the hem of his robe were small bells that would make noise as he moved about performing his duties in the holy of holies (Exod. 28:33–35). The last part of verse 35 says, "The sound of the bells will be heard when he enters the Holy Place before the LORD and when he comes out, so that he will not die." How drastic! The bells were necessary to let the other priests know if the high priest was still alive as he stood in the presence of the Lord.

Tradition also tells us that a rope was tied around the high priest's waist in case he died while he stood before the ark of the presence of God. The other priests, who waited in the holy place, could pull on the rope to bring him out without having to go inside. Entering the holy of holies was something of the gravest importance and could not be taken lightly.

Those who entered the holy place were required to do so with the utmost respect, following stringent guidelines. The Bible relates the account of one person who failed to follow these rules. King Uzziah was a man who began well, but ended badly. Many of the things he did were good, but he became more and more prideful as he became more and more powerful (2 Chron. 26:16).

In this attitude of pride, one day he entered the temple to burn incense on the altar. The altar of incense was not in the holy of holies—but it was in the holy place. While he was there, Azariah, the chief priest, came in and warned him about the mistake he was making.

The king became angry at the priest, obviously believing it unnecessary for him to follow the protocol of priests for coming before God. It didn't matter to him that only Levitical priests were allowed to offer sacrifices. He must have thought that all his good deeds gave him special privileges and access to God.

Wrong! Right there before the priests, God judged him, afflicting him with leprosy. King Uzziah left humiliated, sick, and dying. What was his legacy? "King Uzziah had leprosy until the day he died. He lived in a separate house—leprous, and excluded from the temple of the LORD" (2 Chron. 26:21).

Imagine the kinds of stories that must have circulated

throughout Israel about what had happened: "The king has been judged by God with leprosy." "Did you hear? The king tried to do the priests' job, and God afflicted him with leprosy." If God afflicts the king—a man of importance and influence in the kingdom—won't He do the same to anyone else who does the same thing? No wonder the people were saying, "I'm glad we don't have the job of dealing with that awesome and powerful God. Let the priests do it!" If something so terrible could happen in the holy place, just imagine the care the high priests took when entering the holy of holies. I don't believe one detail would have been omitted.

The sons of Eli are another example of those who became careless with the things pertaining to the tabernacle and were subjected to God's judgment. (See 1 Samuel 2:12–25.) These men surely had ample opportunity to get things right with God, but since they never changed their merciless way of living, the Bible says, " . . . it was the LORD's will to put them to death" (v. 25).

As a result of these stories, plus the things commonly known by the people about what went on in and around the tabernacle, I think a fear was instilled in the people for anything having to do with God and His holy place. I believe this fear continues until this day. Most people are happy staying at the "gates" of the tabernacle and letting the priests go in "before God." This mentality has deep roots in many people, especially those with a background that elevates the office of ministry and implants the idea that only someone with a special inroad to God is allowed to make intercession for us.

Christ, while still nailed on the cross, exclaimed, "It is finished." The veil in the temple that separated the holy of holies was torn from top to bottom (Matt. 27:51). God provided through Jesus free access to the throne of God for *all* believers. Jesus is now our High Priest, and He makes intercession for us, having offered Himself as the last expiation, once and for all, for every man, woman, boy, and girl (Heb. 4:14). Now it's up to us to begin to have the confidence to enter before His throne because of Jesus, and thus develop a deeper and more intimate relationship with Him.

It is important to understand that God sees us *through Jesus*. Everyone who draws near to Him will be given an audience. Consider this:

> For we do not have a high priest who is unable to sympathize with our weaknesses, but we have one who has been tempted in every way, just as we are—yet was without sin. Let us then approach the throne of grace with confidence, so that we may receive mercy and find grace to help us in our time of need.
>
> —HEBREWS 4:15–16

The worshiper who is seeking the Father is the one who knows and understands that we have to go before the throne of God with care. It is not a game. We have to enter by way of our High Priest, Jesus Christ, but we can do so with confidence. We shouldn't fear His presence in the negative sense of the word *fear,* but we must realize that His presence is awesome and give Him the reverence, respect, and honor He deserves. Worshiping is much more than singing songs about Christ sitting on the throne of our lives—it is allowing Him to reside there every day of our lives. *Worship is a way of life.*

Allow the bulldozer of the Holy Spirit
to break you, and then to renew,
restore, mold, and make you anew.
He does such a beautiful job of restoration
and purification. Let Him start on you.

Six

—

An Encounter With God

See pg 97, 99

BEING A TRUE WORSHIPER HAS VERY LITTLE TO DO WITH SINGING songs and playing music—it involves communion with God and developing a relationship with Him.

Worshiping God is not a method; it doesn't require following some simple rules, playing certain notes on an instrument, or singing certain songs or hymns. *It has to do with having an encounter with God.*

There is a passage in the Bible that shows us very clearly what happens when we dare to have an encounter with God:

> In the year that King Uzziah died, I saw the Lord seated on a throne, high and exalted, and the train of his robe filled the temple. Above him were seraphs, each with six wings: With two wings they covered their faces, with two they covered their feet, and with two they were flying. And they were calling to

83

one another: "Holy, holy, holy is the LORD Almighty; the whole earth is full of his glory." At the sound of their voices the doorposts and thresholds shook and the temple was filled with smoke. "Woe to me!" I cried. "I am ruined! For I am a man of unclean lips, and I live among a people of unclean lips, and my eyes have seen the King, the LORD Almighty."

Then one of the seraphs flew to me with a live coal in his hand, which he had taken with tongs from the altar. With it he touched my mouth and said, "See, this has touched your lips; your guilt is taken away and your sin atoned for."

Then I heard the voice of the Lord saying, "Whom shall I send? And who will go for us?"

And I said, "Here am I. Send me!"

He said, "Go and tell this people . . ."

—ISAIAH 6:1–9

In this chapter we are going to take a closer look at some of the things that happened in this incredible encounter, which can serve as an example of worship.

"I SAW THE LORD"

ONE THING THAT STANDS OUT IN ISAIAH'S ENCOUNTER WITH THE Lord is the realness of the encounter in every sense of the word. Isaiah did not have some kind of nightmare; he did not see a vision or experience some aberration of indigestion as a result of eating too much pizza the night before. It was not a product of his imagination, either. The prophet was not making up some kind of supernatural encounter—he experienced a real, life-changing encounter with God. "The doorposts and thresholds shook," and "the temple was filled with smoke."

Many people have had encounters with God over the years—some genuine, while others were no more than emotional encounters.

84

I am a fourth-generation preacher on my mother's side and a third-generation preacher on my father's side. I grew up in the church as a member of a minister's family. Growing up, there were always people in our home, either from our church or from the different congregations that my parents helped found.

As far back as I can remember, I have attended services and observed how people respond to the gospel and to the presence of God. I have seen many "encounters" with God. A lot of these "encounters" have been nothing more than an overflow of emotions, while others have been real and true encounters with the Lord.

One of the surest proofs that a man or woman has had an encounter with God is the change it produces in that life. How many times have we seen people go to the altar, shed tears, pray for a long time, and show all kinds of signs of having an encounter with God—yet they get up from their knees, go back home, and never change a thing? I would dare say that these people have not had a *true* encounter. Perhaps what they had was an emotional encounter. But an emotional encounter with God will not change your life; only a true encounter with God can do that.

There are examples of men in the Bible who had true encounters with God. Jacob was a young man who loved the things of God, more so than did his brother Esau. His name means "supplanter," which means to "occupy someone else's place." There are many "supplanters" in this life. People who want to get ahead at someone else's expense. These people play dirty in order to take advantage of someone else.

Jacob, the "supplanter," played a trick on his brother one day, which caused some pretty big trouble. (See Genesis 25–33.)

When Jacob found it necessary to flee from his home, he went to live with his uncle, Laban. They turned out to be two peas in a pod—his uncle was as bad, or worse, than Jacob as far as tricks were concerned.

After many years filled with "supplantings," Jacob, now a prosperous and blessed man, decided to return to his homeland. While on the road home with many servants, cattle, and possessions, he received the news that his brother was coming to meet him—with four hundred armed men. Esau was going to get his revenge for the trick Jacob played on him so many years before.

At that moment, Jacob realized one thing: He needed God! Many times the Lord allows certain things to happen in our lives to bring us to the point where we realize that without Him we are nothing and that we desperately need His help. This happened to Jacob.

In chapter 32 of Genesis, Jacob had a true encounter with God. He wrestled with the angel of the Lord all night until the dawn, when he told the angel, "I will not let you go unless you bless me" (32:26). The "man" finally blessed Jacob, but not before doing two things: First he changed Jacob's name to *Israel*. The broader meaning of the word *Israel* means "God prevails." But the word *Israel* comes from two root words: *sara,* which means "to contend with, persist, exert oneself," and *el,* which is the word for God.

From these meanings we remember each time we hear the word *Israel* that Jacob "struggled with God." And since Jacob did not let go until the angel of the Lord had blessed him, we can deduce that he is a man who, out of his struggle with God, received what he wanted from God. Thus he is called "Israel"! How incredible! From that day on his name remained as a testament to having had a true encounter with God.

The second thing the angel did to Jacob was to wound his hip. I can just see Jacob after that historic night in his life, limping back to camp and being asked, "Jacob, what happened?"

To which he quickly responded, "My name is no longer *Jacob,* but *Israel*: 'God Prevails.'"

From that day on, when anyone asked him why he

limped, he could tell them it was because he had an encounter with God. Note what I am going to say: When we have a *true* encounter with God, *even the way we walk changes.*

When Jacob asked the "man" he had been struggling with what his name was, he received only this answer: "Why do you ask my name?" But then the man blessed him, a sign that Jacob had indeed been in the presence of the Lord God Almighty.

Jacob called the place *Peniel,* which means "facing God." Then Jacob, or rather Israel, exclaimed: "I saw God face to face, and yet *my life was spared*" (vv. 27–30, emphasis added). Jacob's words remind us of the words spoken by Isaiah in chapter 6 of his book.

There is one thing that puzzles me to this day. Jacob had previously had an interesting experience with God at Bethel, but it hadn't changed the way he lived. (See Genesis 28:10–22.) At Bethel, when he was fleeing from his home, he had a wonderful dream and even a word of promise from God. But it wasn't the same as the encounter he had at Peniel. After Peniel, we see a totally different Jacob—a more spiritual Jacob—a Jacob who knows more about who God is.

Israel becomes a patriarch of the faith, assured, stable—everything he hadn't been before Peniel. This is a great lesson about the importance of having a true encounter with God. Emotional experiences may have some purpose; like Jacob at Bethel, we may make some sort of commitment as the result of an emotional experience. But what completely transforms us forever is the encounter we have at our Peniel.

We all have the need to be able to say, "I saw the Lord." The only way we can is if we have a true encounter with God. It's time to stop playing "church" and do as David did: It's time "to seek him in his temple" (Ps. 27:4). Then, with Isaiah, Israel, and David, we will be able to say, "I saw the Lord."

Spiritual blindness is something that weighs down all of us. We need to ask the Lord to open our eyes so that we can see Him. The apostle Paul wrote to the Ephesians: "I keep asking that the God of our Lord Jesus Christ . . . may give you the Spirit of wisdom and revelation" (Eph. 1:17). Paul knew that one of the biggest problems in the church is not being able to see in the spirit what is going on around us.

In the Old Testament, Elisha had a similar problem with one of his servants, and he prayed: "O LORD, open his eyes so he may see" (2 Kings 6:17). One reason the church today has no power or direction and carries a weak testimony in the world is that we can't say as Isaiah said, "I saw the Lord." We are so busy trying to solve the church's problems from a human, secular point of view that we forget to "inquire" of Him, to know what His direction is for a given situation. It is time we asked the Lord to open the eyes of our understanding so that we can see Him, so that we may be changed into His image and likeness. Maybe then we will be able to do things the way He does them.

"WOE TO ME!"

I DON'T KNOW WHAT YOU WOULD HAVE SAID UPON FINDING yourself in a situation similar to Isaiah's, but I think you probably would have said something similar to what he said: "Woe to me! I am ruined!" When we dare to enter His presence and behold Him, seeing Him in all His glory, magnificence, majesty, beauty, purity, holiness, justice, and perfection, we come face to face with the sad reality of our state: We are completely the opposite!

In the light of His presence, we can see all those things in our lives that go against His desires and purposes for us. Suddenly, by being in His presence and being confronted with His perfection, we will recognize the changes needed in our lives.

Many times we have been in places with poor lighting where we can't see very well. Maybe it was a restaurant where, to create a certain "atmosphere," the lights are low. Invariably, while eating in a place like that we will spill some food on our clothing—especially those of us who wear ties. Ties seem to be magnets for food. Somehow your food, or mine, or maybe both, will wind up on my tie.

Sitting there in an ill-lit place, I take a napkin and "clean" the food off my tie. After inspecting it under the poor lighting I think, *Well, I've solved that little problem; my tie is now clean.*

But later when I go to the restroom where the lighting is much better, I realize that the problem has not been fixed at all, but it is still very much there. So I take a little towel, wet it, and begin "cleaning" my tie. Now, in that improved light, I think: *Now everything is fixed.* Still later I get up and walk out into the midday sun, look at my tie, and what do you think? The problem is far from being resolved! Suddenly I realize a much more serious problem exists. Not only is the original stain there, but now all the other stains added by my efforts to "fix" the problem are also there. All I really did was extend the stain over a larger area of my tie. I only made the problem worse. I should have sent the tie to the cleaners instead of trying to get it clean by myself.

The same thing happens when we come before the Lord in His perfect light. If we try to measure things by the earthly, worldly light, we are never going to be done with the problem of sin in our lives. We have to go into His presence and allow His light to shine on our lives, showing us the things that are not right, and then we allow Him to change them. This is what happened to Isaiah. Instead of talking about the changes coming in the kingdom and polling people about what they thought about the king dying at the hand of God, the prophet knew that the only way he could obtain answers to his questions was by going into the presence of God. But God's judgment had to come before anything else could happen. Many people avoid God's presence because they know His light will reveal many disagreeable things that need to be changed in their lives. Thus they fail to become true worshipers.

"Woe to me! I am ruined" is also an exclamation of humility before a great King. I believe Isaiah had not thought about what he was going to say when he yelled out these words—it was a heartfelt cry that came from the certainty that God could strike him down any moment because of the sin in his life. Perhaps he yelled these words in hopes of obtaining mercy; immediately after crying out, he confessed his sin in complete recognition of his need to change. The man or woman who knows God's presence is someone who knows how to quickly confess error and ask for mercy. The stubborn or obstinate person is the one who says that everything is all right. Entering into God's presence makes us sensitive, open, and vulnerable—characteristics of a true worshiper.

Second Chronicles 7:14 says, "If my people, who are called by my name, will humble themselves and pray and seek my face and turn from their wicked ways, then will I hear from heaven and will forgive their sin and will heal their land." Notice that it doesn't say, "If the nations of the earth . . . " It says, "If *my* people . . . "

As the people of the Lord, we have to go into His presence, admit the sins among us, and allow Him to cleanse us of those sins so He can heal our land. Many "lands" have not been healed because the Lord's people are more interested in singing their precious songs and playing their lovely music—which are not in themselves bad—than in getting down on their faces and humbling themselves before the King of kings and allowing Him to change them as only He can.

Will there be those who are willing to say, "Woe to me!

I am ruined!" as a result of being in His presence and seeing Him? Who will go into the Lord's sanctuary, allow His light to shine on their lives, and be changed by Him?

"Then One of the Seraphims Flew to Me" *THE PRICE we have must pay*

After acknowledging his problem, Isaiah was ready for the next step—which is also the most painful part of the encounter: the purification process. It is necessary to go through this process before God can use us. The Bible speaks of this process many times, imploring us not to get impatient because the work of the Lord in our lives will be perfected. We need to "see" the global picture of what He is doing—this is an essential step that must be completed before we can go on.

I can only imagine what Isaiah thought as that seraph began to fly toward him. He must have been thinking: *What is that seraph going to do with that live coal?* Probably, as the seraph got closer and closer, Isaiah realized that the seraph was going to touch him with it. Isaiah had two options at that moment: Cooperate with the move of God in his life and allow the seraph to do what it had to do, or he could brusquely terminate the process (as we have done so many times just when the Lord is ready to deal with certain things in our lives) by getting up from that place and saying, "Okay, Lord, well . . . I think I need to go and minister to your children who most certainly need me right now." Quickly, before that mean ol' seraph could reach him, he could have run out from the Lord's presence. He could have thought, *Everything was going so smoothly until that crazy seraph ruined it all.* Isaiah chose the first option—he was serious about what was going on.

Many modern-day Christians flee from God's presence by staying in the outer courts and singing many beautiful and true songs. But by our lifestyles we make it obvious that we don't live what we sing. For example, how many of us have sung, "Change my heart, Oh God; make it ever true"? Do we really mean it? When the Lord wants to begin a renewal process, do we allow Him to do so? The song continues, "You are the potter; I am the clay. Mold me and make me; this is what I pray."[1] One fine day the Lord is going to take us at our word, and He's going to begin to mold us.

A bulldozer is an enormous machine with a huge shovel on the front to level things and some claws (like a fork) on the back that are used to dig. Use your imagination with me for a moment. One day as we are singing, "Change my heart, Oh God . . . ," we suddenly cry out, "Lord, what's that big thing coming toward me?"

The Lord answers, "It's a bulldozer."

We respond, "O-o-oh. So . . . what are You going to do with that thing?"

The Lord answers, "Well, I'm going to change your heart."

"Lord, don't You think You're being a little bit drastic?" we ask hurriedly. "The shovel on that thing is really big, and I don't think I have *that* much sin."

The Lord replies, "But, for a long time you have been singing, 'Mold me, make me . . . ' and all those things. So I brought this machine so that we can fix what needs to be fixed once and for all."

Suddenly you exclaim, "But those are only songs, Lord. Wow! You sure do take things literally! That's just the way we sing at our church."

The noise of the machine can still be heard. As it begins to sweep over us we cry out in pain, "Ouch! That really hurts, Lord."

Gently the Lord answers, "Yes, I know. That is why I have given you My Word. Listen to this: 'Never will I leave you; never will I forsake you' (Heb. 13:5). And I have promised this: 'No temptation has seized you except what is common to man. And God is faithful; he will not let you be tempted beyond what you can bear. But when you are tempted, he will also provide a way out so that you can stand up under it' (1 Cor. 10:13)."

So, with His help, we stand up under the shovel's excavation. Just when we think it's over, we glance behind and see the huge fork claws in the back. Panicked again, we cry, "Lord, what's going on?"

Again the Lord replies, "We need to get to the root of the problem and take it out so that it will never come up in your life again."

That's the molding process. That's the result of singing "dangerous" songs, inviting God to "change my heart, Oh God." The purification process starts when God takes you up on what you have sung so many times. If you want to be a true worshiper, you have to go through the purification process. Don't run from it! Face it, once and for all! Allow the bulldozer of the Holy Spirit to break you, and then to renew, restore, mold, and make you anew. He does such a beautiful job of restoration and purification. Let Him start on you.

We can see this purification process take place in the life of Paul. Paul had the right perspective on the pain of renewal. He said:

> For our light and momentary troubles are achieving
> for us an eternal glory that far outweighs them all.
> —2 CORINTHIANS 4:17

Paul's problems, the things he endured in his lifetime, hardly seem like "light and momentary troubles." Paul went through some things that you and I have never gone through. In 2 Corinthians 11, Paul lists some of his difficulties. Let's take a look at just a few of the "light and momentary" troubles that he lived through. He was:

- in prison frequently (v. 23).
- flogged severely more than once (v. 23).
- exposed to death again and again (v. 23).

- beaten five times, each time receiving thirty-nine lashes from the Jews (v. 24).
- beaten three times with rods (v. 25).
- stoned once (v. 25).
- shipwrecked three times (v. 25).
- left stranded for a night and a day in the open sea (v. 25).
- forced to live his life on the run (v. 26).
- endangered by rivers, bandits, his own countrymen, Gentiles, and false brothers (v. 26).
- not safe in cities, in the country, or at sea (v. 26).
- often forced to work hard; often deprived of his basic needs (v. 27).

This is a partial list of the "light and momentary" afflictions the apostle Paul had to experience in order to achieve "an eternal glory that far outweighs them all" (2 Cor. 4:17). He was willing to go through whatever it took to "know Christ and the power of his resurrection and the fellowship of sharing in his sufferings, becoming like him in his death" (Phil. 3:10).

Paul wanted to become like Christ. That must also be our desire. Like Paul, we must be willing to share "in his sufferings," willing to confront even death to experience the resurrection power (Phil 3:11).

I don't recall anyone ever coming up to me and saying, "Marcos, I want to become like Jesus; I am willing for Him to put me through any kind of test if only I can know Him." Most people are trying to *get rid* of their problems—they're not looking for more "tests." But Paul had learned that all the adverse things he endured served to achieve "an eternal glory." How amazing! He understood that everything serves but one purpose in our lives: To produce the glory of Christ in us.

Even though at times we may experience a time of testing and a situation that is very hard to understand or bear, we can be confident in the truth that God is working all things in our lives for good (Rom. 8:28). If only we could have the same kind of vision Paul had as he wrote about his "light and momentary" afflictions. Then we would welcome the purification process in our lives—rather than opposing it.

Often the work that God is completing in our individual lives is connected to the global picture of what the Lord wants to do. Because we get so caught up in the "here and now," we lose out on the importance of seeing things as the Lord sees them: globally. Don't forget that He can see the past and the future. We see only the past and the present, and we are most affected by what we are experiencing at this moment. We get caught up with lamenting our present situation, without realizing that what happens now can have a very positive effect on the future. The Lord, who sees all things, allows things to happen now to prepare us for the future. By having "global vision" we can rest in the Lord, trusting that He is working everything for our good.

"Then I Heard the Voice of the Lord"

The use of the word *then* in verse 8 of Isaiah 6 intrigues me. It probably means that the purification process had to be completed *before* Isaiah was able to discern and hear the voice of the Lord. The Lord has not stopped speaking today, and many of us want to hear His voice and receive direction for our lives.

Isaiah helps us understand the reason that we don't hear the Lord's voice is not because He is no longer speaking, but because we are so busy listening to other things that we can't hear Him. The Lord constantly speaks to us about our families, congregations, jobs, neighbors, countries, and everything else. He has the answer or solution to every problem or challenge that we might be facing today. The problem isn't Him—it's us. We can't hear!

We are like the man walking down the street with a banana in his ear. Another gentleman sees him and thinks, *I am going to tell that man he has a banana in his ear.* He comes up to the man with the banana in his ear and says, "Excuse me, sir. I just wanted to tell you that you have a banana in your ear."

The other man answers, "Pardon?"

More loudly, the first man answers, "I just wanted to tell you about the banana in your ear."

The man with the banana asks, "What did you say?"

By this time the first man is speaking in a very loud voice. "I felt obliged to tell you that you have a banana in your ear. You need to take care of it."

The man with the banana replies, "I'm sorry, sir; you will have to speak a lot louder because I have this banana in my ear!"

That's how many of us are. We pray, "Lord, I need You to speak much louder because there are so many other things I have to listen to also." We need to submit to the purifying process, allowing the Lord to clean all those other voices out of our spiritual ears so we can hear only His voice.

Radio, television, and other means of communication work on frequencies. Certain frequencies are designated for radio and others for television. To be able to listen to our favorite program, we have to tune in to the frequency that is transmitting the program. Hundreds of things are being said and done at any given moment, but we see or hear only that to which we are tuned. It's the same way with the Holy Spirit. We need to change frequencies and stop listening to so many other things; we need to "tune in" to the Holy Spirit's frequency.

"Here Am I; Send Me!"

When someone knows the Lord's voice, the immediate and certain answer to it is, "Here am I. Send me!" This is another characteristic of someone who has experienced the presence of the Lord as the prophet did on this occasion. There is not one moment of hesitation—only an affirmative, enthusiastic response.

Why then do so many Christians, upon knowing the Lord's direction for their lives, fail to give an affirmative answer? We take our time, we delay, and at our convenience we respond, if it is something that comes naturally to us. There are so many times the Lord wants to use us, but we have failed to take the progressive steps I've outlined in this chapter. We don't take the time to see the Lord seated upon a throne, high and exalted; we do not acknowledge our faults; and we do not unplug our ears to hear the clear, concise voice of the Lord. As a result, the Lord passes us by and seeks another person who *will* listen to Him, and He uses that person instead.

The words of the psalmist David are a challenge to us. He asserted: "My heart is steadfast, O God" (Ps. 57:7; 108:1). The word *steadfast* in Hebrew has the connotation of something that is prepared, established, always ready, and willing. This is the way every person who knows the presence of the Lord should be. Someone who is ready "in season and out of season" (2 Tim. 4:2).

One of the ways we can measure our willingness is by how we respond to the people God has put around us. Do you respond willingly when volunteers are needed? Do you support your pastors and leaders? Check your level of willingness—it's a good clue to your progression to becoming a true worshiper. There should not be a shortage of volunteers in our churches—the opposite should be true: There should be an abundance of people ready and willing to do something for the Lord.

Isaiah's quick response to the Lord was: "Send me!" This is another characteristic of someone who has been with the Lord: That person can't picture God having to use someone else. Those who say, "Here I am, Lord; send *him*," quickly committing the other person (something that is so easy to do), have obviously not been in His presence. If they have been in His presence, they would not want to miss out on the wonderful opportunity of God's using them, no matter the cost.

This person has already paid the high price of purification—the question of costs has already been resolved. As a result, it is easy, almost automatic to answer, "Send me." Isaiah, and others like him, have nurtured a relationship with God; they are confident that the task to which the Lord assigns them will be something exciting, challenging, and totally invigorating. They wouldn't want to miss it for anything in the world!

This is what is so sad about people who have not nurtured this kind of relationship: They miss out on thousands of opportunities to be used by God. No wonder there are so many bored, tired, and frustrated Christians out there! They haven't gone into the temple to see the Lord and set into motion the changes that will make them into people who respond dynamically and enthusiastically to the work of the Lord!

"He Said . . ."

FINALLY, HERE IT IS! ISAIAH WAS ABOUT TO RECEIVE WHAT MANY want to have without first having to go through the steps we have been talking about. He was to receive a task. Many are more interested in the tasks than in the God who distributes the tasks. Sometimes, in an attempt "to be used" by God for whatever reasons, we find ourselves fighting for posts and positions. "This is MY ministry . . ." or "This is MY place."

The need for position, recognition, and prestige is often equated with "doing" the tasks the Lord gives out. But we are so wrong! Paul writes to the Corinthians: "Therefore I will boast all the more gladly about my weaknesses, so that Christ's power may rest on me" (2 Cor. 12:9). In his first epistle to the Corinthians, he had written, "For who makes you different from anyone else? What do you have that you did not receive? And if you did receive it, why do you boast as though you did not?" (1 Cor. 4:7). Strong words, words that demand commitment. We should never think that the "tasks" we do for the Lord are more important than He is. Our first priority is to be with Him and to get to know Him. The result of knowing Him will be the acknowledging of the error of our ways, the refining of the purification process, and the ability to hear God's voice and respond quickly; only then will we receive the task He has chosen to give to us.

We can live according to this pattern on a daily basis. If we are interested in doing the Lord's will, then we need to enter the sanctuary and *"see the Lord"* before we begin to "do" what He wants us to do. We must first become true worshipers, passing through each of the processes I have written about in this chapter.

- See the Lord and spend time with Him.
- Repent.
- Pass through the purification process.
- Hear the Word of the Lord.
- Respond to His voice,
- Receive His instructions.
- Do His work.

Are you ready to make this commitment?

Do not glorify Him as some great teacher
or as a "supreme being who lives in the
cosmos of eternity"—glorify Him as God,
the Lord of hosts who rules the heavens
with power and glory, and in His right
hand forever are justice and equity. Let
there be no mistake: He is God! And
as such, He must be glorified.

Seven

The Importance of
Praising and Worshiping

*I*PRAY THAT BY NOW THE LORD HAS AWAKENED A GREAT DESIRE
in your heart to be a true worshiper and that you have
taken the steps to obtain your goal. It will be important to
maintain an attitude of thankfulness, praise, and worship
in our lives. Romans chapter 1 helps us understand how
to do that.

> The wrath of God is being revealed from heaven
> against all the godlessness and wickedness of men
> who suppress the truth by their wickedness, since
> what may be known about God is plain to them,
> because God has made it plain to them. For since
> the creation of the world God's invisible qualities—
> his eternal power and divine nature—have been
> clearly seen, being understood from what has been
> made, so that men are without excuse.
>
> —ROMANS 1:18–20

This passage verifies that God has put within every man and woman a consciousness of His existence, which is why His wrath is ignited when we stop His truth with injustice. The language is emphatic—it leaves no room for doubt. Paul says, "So that men are without excuse."

It is impossible to look around at God's creation— observing the stars in the sky, experiencing the ocean's majesty, listening to the wind blowing through the trees in a great forest, enjoying the birds singing, and observing the sparkle of a hillside stream—and still say there is no God. Only a fool would dare say there is no God, just as the psalmist says.

Paul states clearly that even those things that cannot be seen by the human eye ("God's invisible qualities") are revealed to us by the things that we can see—His creation and His works. He emphasizes this by saying such things are "understood." He leaves no room for misunderstanding that we all have some knowledge of God. Therefore we have no excuse to live in the ways of sin that Paul goes on to describe in this passage. Let's take a look at the list:

- injustice
- perversion
- evil
- murder
- deceit
- gossip
- God-haters
- arrogance
- senselessness
- ruthlessness
- disobedience to their parents
- heartlessness; without natural affection
- fornication
- greed
- envy
- strife
- malice
- slander
- insolence
- boastfulness
- faithlessness
- inventing ways to do evil

Doesn't this list remind you of the morning newspaper or the news broadcast you watched last night? Doesn't it describe perfectly the society in which we live today?

How did we sink to these levels of depravity? How is it that the murderer has the gall, the indecency, the effrontery to take a fellow human's life? How could the adulterer dare to sleep with his best friend's wife, or the young man to steal a young lady's virginity in a moment of passion and lust?

Did you notice that it said, "They invent ways to do evil"? How is it possible that there are those who *dedicate* themselves to inventing evil, ugly things, spending a large part of their lives trying to think up new ways to destroy their fellow human beings, bringing shame to the human race? How can so many people be an affront to the God of the universe? How is it that pride rules the heart of man? When did deceit and evil enter his thoughts?

Do you think that it was something that happened overnight? Did the murderer wake up one day, look in the mirror, and say to himself, *I think this is a good day to go out and kill somebody*? Does the adulterer wake up one morning and say, "Hey! How did I wake up in my neighbor's wife's bed?" Do disobedience, lying, disloyalty, and even homosexuality happen merely because people are "out of control"? How did gossip and murmuring become a part of our lives? Was it purely accidental and thus a product of "fate"?

The answer to these questions is that all these things are the *product of a process*. It is a process that is clearly explained in the first chapter of Romans, but we have overlooked it so many times. Let's go back to the beginning and see what brought our society down to the depths it is in today.

THE PROCESS THAT LEADS DOWNWARD

THE FIRST STEP DOWN TO DEPRAVITY IS FOUND IN ROMANS 1:21: "For although they knew God, they neither glorified him as God...." There it is. The first step downward is not giving God the glory of which He is worthy. According to the dictionary, the word *glorify* means to "honor, celebrate, exalt, praise; call to enjoy heavenly blessings." By not glorifying Him as God—praising, worshiping, celebrating, and glorifying Him—we begin the spiral downward into the sins described in verses 29 to 31. Failing to glorify God causes us to take for ourselves the place that rightfully belongs to Him, and this is very dangerous. What is the result? Read verses 29 to 31 again and you will see.

Not only are we to glorify God—we are to glorify Him *as* God (v. 21). The Bible teaches that God is jealous (Exod. 20:5; 34:14; Deut. 4:24). He does not share His glory with anyone. We have to glorify Him for who He is: the God of all creation, omnipotent Creator who was, and is, and is to come. We cannot glorify Him as just another deity or person. He is God, and outside of Him there is no other deity. Do not glorify Him as some great teacher or as a "supreme being who lives in the cosmos of eternity"—glorify Him as God, the Lord of hosts who rules the heavens with power and glory, and in His right hand forever are justice and equity. Let there be no mistake: *He is God!* And as such, He must be glorified.

The second step in the journey downward is also found in verse 21: "Nor gave thanks to him." It is important to live a life of thankfulness to the Lord. Living in a constant state of thankfulness to Him, in everything and for everything, is one of the things that will keep us from falling. This second step of ceasing to be thankful is a direct result of the first step. If I am not glorifying Him as God, then it is easy to come to the conclusion that I do not have to thank Him. Why should I thank Someone who is not in control of my life and who may not even exist for me? That is the reasoning of a person who has not established who God is and what place He occupies in their life. Ungratefulness is the sign of a person who has drifted away from God.

If you and I cannot acknowledge from whom things come and can't remember that His goodness and mercy *w/e (might) one puffed up*

1 Cor.en 4:6-7

are much more than we deserve, then it will be very easy for us to fall into the next step downward: Ungratefulness. This is why it is vitally important that we glorify Him and add a spirit of continual gratefulness to our lifestyle, because it keeps us correctly focused on the fact that everything we have is because of Him. Nothing we have is ours because of our own strength; everything is from Him. He will watch over and protect us because He is firmly seated on the throne. *He* is in control, not *us*.

③ The third step in the progressive spiral downward is this: "Their thinking became futile..." (v. 21). Can you see what a natural sequence this is? If we fail to glorify God, soon we will also cease giving Him thanks for His blessings. As we cease thanking Him, we will also cease acknowledging that all things come from Him and that we have nothing of ourselves. From that point, it is very easy, almost automatic, to develop the attitude that our way of thinking is the best. Why should we believe the reasoning of a God whom we have not allowed to be the ruler of our thoughts?

If we have not first established these important steps in our lives, then how easy it is to begin believing that our thoughts are superior ones. We begin coming to our own individual conclusions. We no longer need the Lord to resolve our problems—we can efficiently work out all the circumstances of this life. So we think, *If you will permit me, Lord, step aside; I don't need You anymore.*

Have you ever been around someone whose thoughts were futile, who was convinced he or she had the answers to the whole world's problems? How does this person make you feel? Don't they seem obstinate and repugnant to you? Isn't it usually an unpleasant experience to be in their presence? We can guard ourselves from this by giving glory and thanks to the one Lord of all.

④ The fourth step in the progression is automatic: "Their foolish hearts were darkened..." (v. 21). When we do not need God or His counsel, we become foolish;

foolishness brings darkness to our hearts. How sad today to see men and women living in spiritual darkness when, by the light of His Word, we can know that Christ has won a wonderful victory for every man, woman, boy, and girl.

We can know that Christ's blood has cleansed us from all sin and that He has offered one single sacrifice for all. People who have not entered into this light are living under the yoke of sin and slavery. The whole world is "without excuse," according to the apostle who wrote Romans, but even sadder are those who, after knowing the light of His salvation, discovering the great treasures of His Word, and experiencing some of the awesome redemption and mercy of the Lord, stop giving Him glory, quit being thankful, become futile in their thoughts, and as a result, end up in spiritual darkness.

Many who "began well" wind up as false prophets— men whom God raised up but who allowed themselves to receive the glory that should have been given to the Lord. They developed a higher concept of themselves than they should have (Rom. 12:3), which led to futile thoughts. They began preaching things without a biblical base and, in this way, deceived thousands and caused disasters in the kingdom.

It is so important to keep our focus on who God is! It is indispensable to glorify and thank Him always! Don't end up in spiritual blindness by failing to give Him glory and thanks. Be careful not to fall into a trap of deceit. Developing an intimate relationship with the Lord will help us to discern when men are teaching things out of their futile thoughts. We will be able to refute them and to know God's heart through His Word and the witness of His Spirit in us.

(5) Once a person's "foolish heart is darkened," the entire being is affected, and the fifth progressive step occurs: "Although they claimed to be wise, they became fools" (v. 22). So many people profess to be wise! Because their thoughts are futile, they declare themselves to be wise,

without realizing they are becoming more and more futile.

The Pharisees are a perfect example of this. They were the spiritual leaders of their day, and they maintained a facade of spirituality, importance, and piety. They thought they had all the answers. They spent their time devising sneaky questions to "trap" Jesus, thus embarrassing Him and getting in good with the crowd. What they obviously did not know was that they were complete fools living in the midst of great spiritual darkness.

There are many modern-day pharisees among us today! Men and women who think they have all the answers. People who think that their "position" in the kingdom or their years of "experience" in the ministry have exempted them of the need of bowing before the throne of God with glory and thanks. They try to solve problems on their own, without consulting the Lord as they did in the early days of ministry.

(6) The final step downward is the collective result of taking all the previous steps: They exchanged the glory of the incorruptible God for images of corruptible men! (See verse 23.) How can this be? Who would dare touch God's glory with the idea of changing it? Who would dare tell us that God's glory is like "mortal man and birds and animals and reptiles"? By this time you probably already know who it is. It is that person who did not give God glory or thanks; whose thoughts became futile; whose darkened heart became foolish; and who became convinced he was greater than God and could do with God what he pleased.

Do you know that even within the church there are many idolaters who, in some way or other, have exchanged the glory of God for something else? Idolatry exists not only in someone who bends the knee to a false deity or image, but in any person who allows something or someone to take precedence over Jesus Christ. There are many people who hold their church or denomination in higher regard than the Lord Jesus, or who love the ministry of the Lord more than the Lord of the ministry. Others place great importance on material goods, like the rich young ruler. Many put more importance on a relationship with family, boyfriend, or girlfriend than on their relationship with Christ.

Be very careful! The result of changing God's glory is a very dangerous one: "God gave them over in the sinful desires of their hearts to sexual impurity" (v. 24). This almost sounds as if God Himself lost hope in us and finally said to Himself, "If they are determined to adhere to their own thoughts and wisdom, and if they don't want to nurture a relationship with Me, if they dare to change My glory for other things, then…go right ahead. But they do it without My blessing or My protection."

Do you want to stand firm, without falling? Give Him glory. Give Him thanks. Do you want to develop a relationship of total dependence on Him? Give Him glory. Give Him thanks. Do you want to begin destroying unfruitful works of the flesh? Give Him glory and thanks. Do not ever tire of putting the Lord in the place where He belongs, the one of complete authority and dominion over your life. Enthrone Him in your life by always giving Him glory and thanks. This can be one of the things that can keep you strong in the faith. Let us never forget the importance of praise, celebration, worship, and thanksgiving in our lives. If you will always keep Him seated firmly on the throne of your life, you will never begin the downward steps to depravity.

Do you want to become a true worshiper? Give Him glory, and give Him thanks!

*E*ach time we raise our hearts to God
in sincerity, love, and dedication,
to exalt, proclaim, and honor His greatness
and His power, we are constructing
a Zion where He can descend
in all His glory upon us.

Eight

Those Who
Dwell in Zion

Many years ago, I heard a preacher say, "You need to be born in Zion." Like so many other times, I wrote that down in the notes I was taking. Later, while looking over my notes, I bumped into that phrase once again. Since I couldn't remember the context in which they were written, I looked up one of the scriptures the preacher had quoted and, what a discovery! I embarked on a very interesting journey, which led me to discover the truth of that phrase. I really need to be born in Zion! And so do you. So, let's begin by going to Psalm 87.

> He has set his foundation on the holy mountain;
>> the LORD loves the gates of Zion
>> more than all the dwellings of Jacob.
> Glorious things are said of you,
>> O city of God:
> "I will record Rahab and Babylon

among those who acknowledge me—
Philistia too, and Tyre, along with Cush—
and will say, 'This one was born in Zion.'"

Indeed, of Zion it will be said,
"This one and that one were born in her,
and the Most High himself will establish her."
The LORD will write in the register of the peoples:
"This one was born in Zion."
As they make music they will sing,
"All my fountains are in you."

The first thing I would like to look at in this psalm is what is said in verse 2: "The LORD loves the gates of Zion more than all the dwellings of Jacob." My first question upon reading verse this was: "What does Zion have that is so special that other dwellings do not have? Why would the Lord love that dwelling more than all the others?" As I explored other passages of Scripture that spoke of Zion, I found something even more interesting—God not only *loves* the gates of Zion, but He also *lives* in Zion. It is His dwelling place. Here are some of the Scriptures that prove this:

Sing praises to the LORD, enthroned in Zion.

—PSALM 9:11

It is beautiful in its loftiness,
the joy of the whole earth.
Like the utmost heights of Zaphon is Mount Zion,
the city of the Great King.

—PSALM 48:2

...Mount Zion, where you dwelt.

—PSALM 74:2

..his dwelling place in Zion.

—PSALM 76:2

But he chose the tribe of Judah,
Mount Zion, which he loved.

—PSALM 78:68

As I searched the Scriptures for an understanding of Zion, the following one impressed me most:

For the LORD has chosen Zion,
he has desired it for his dwelling.

—PSALM 132:13

This indicates that the Lord had a choice as to His dwelling place. He could have chosen any place He wanted as a place to live; however, He chose Zion. I can imagine the Lord looking over all His options for a dwelling place. Certainly some of them were very attractive, but nothing could compare to Zion, and so He chose to live there. What could have made the Lord want Zion as His dwelling place? What were the things He was looking for in a dwelling place?

I wanted to know what the place where the Lord lives was like—it must be a pretty impressive place. I wanted to know why.

You and I live in a materialistic generation, and we've learned that we don't have to settle for just one option of anything; human consumerism has given us an infinite variety of choices. We don't have to be satisfied with anything because pretty soon someone will show up with a better option.

In most cities there are areas of the community that are known for different things. For example, the areas where all the wealthy people live have all the beauty and luxury money can buy. Then you have all the areas where the middle, lower, working, and any other classes live, and each area has identifying characteristics.

When a new development is opened up, all the positive things about it are advertised. Huge billboards proclaim how the neighborhood will look when it is finished. Can you imagine how many lots would sell in a development that could claim it was "the place God chose to dwell"? There wouldn't be enough lots to go around. Everybody would want the lot next to His. The Zion development...A very interesting place...God's dwelling.

We are going to look at some of the things that make Zion such a special place.

WHAT DISTINGUISHES ZION?

ONE OF THE MANY PASSAGES THAT SHED SOME LIGHT ON ZION IS Jeremiah 31:12.

> They will come and shout for joy on the heights of Zion;
> they will rejoice in the bounty of the Lord—
> the grain, the new wine and the oil,
> the young of the flocks and herds.
> They will be like a well-watered garden,
> and they will sorrow no more.

No wonder the Lord liked this place! Just look at all it offers.

1. There is bread in Zion.

One of the biblical symbolisms of *bread* is *the satisfaction of all our physical needs*. There is never hunger in Zion because there is always bread—the divine, daily provision of bread for each inhabitant. ("Give us this day our daily bread....")

The Lord has promised to supply His children's needs. On one occasion David writes, "I was young and now I am old, yet I have never seen the righteous forsaken or their children begging bread" (Ps. 37:25). The apostle Paul tells us, "My God will meet all your needs according to his glorious riches in Christ Jesus" (Phil. 4:19).

We have a God who is interested in the natural, physical needs of each and every one of His children, and He will not forsake them. Matthew says, "Look at the birds of the air; they do not sow or reap or store away in barns, and yet your heavenly Father feeds them. Are you not much more valuable than they?" (Matt. 6:26). Of course you are. God will make sure that each inhabitant of Zion has a portion of daily bread and is well nourished.

2. There is wine in Zion.

On many occasions in the Bible, *wine* is used to signify *happiness, joy, and rejoicing*. Wine was used at celebrations and festivities. When Jesus visited a wedding in Cana, in John chapter 2, He joined the festivities and saved them from an embarrassing situation by changing water into wine. After the great visitation of the Holy Spirit to the upper room on the Day of Pentecost, and everyone began speaking in other tongues, the crowd outside thought they were drunk with wine (Acts 2:15). They must have been making quite a racket for everyone to have thought they were drunk! They probably were shouting, clapping, singing, and laughing just as drunk people do.

Have you ever noticed how a drunk person has a certain "atmosphere" about him? Usually one with lots of music, lots of company (the drunk makes a stranger his best friend), lots of laughter, and lots of courage (he will stand up to anyone and isn't afraid of them).

The apostle Paul admonishes us not to be drunk with wine but to be filled with the Holy Spirit (Eph. 5:18). This verse implies that being drunk in the Spirit produces some of the same effects as being drunk with natural wine. There is enough spiritual wine in Zion for all of her citizens. There is enough of the joy of the Lord so as to be able to share it with others—at no additional cost! No wonder Zion is a place that pleases God: There is joy, happiness, and rejoicing. There is music, dancing, and song. I think God knows how to have a better time than a lot of us do! Zion is a festive, happy place.

3. There is oil in Zion.

We see various applications in the Bible for oil. Let's look at two.

Oil is symbolic of the anointing of the Holy Spirit. Each one of us needs the outpouring of the oil in our lives to be able to move in the strength and power of the Spirit and not in our own. Each one of us needs the oil of His Spirit to make the fire of the candlestick burn in us, just as it did in Moses' tabernacle. Now that we are the dwelling and tabernacle of God, and now that He lives in our hearts, there should be a continuous supply of oil in our holy place so that we can walk in the light of His Holy Spirit.

Jesus said that He would send the Comforter to teach all things and to remind us of all the teachings of our Lord (John 14:26). We all need the presence of the oil of the Holy Spirit to be able to walk in His light. There is plenty of oil for the anointing in Zion.

Oil is also symbolic of the healing that is for all. Oil, in the Bible, speaks of healing. When the good Samaritan treated the wounded man, he used oil and wine.

Jeremiah 8:22 says, "Is there no balm in Gilead? Is there no physician there? Why then is there no healing for the wound of my people?" Balm was an oil that was poured into wounds to aid the healing process. What a wonderful application for the citizens of Zion! In Zion there is healing for every illness. It is only a matter of receiving it, because the oil flows freely in Zion. The sweet balm of the Lord flows over the wounds of each one of Zion's inhabitants, bringing rest and healing. No wonder the Lord "desired" Zion for His dwelling place! What a wonderfully special place. Don't you agree?

4. In Zion we see "the young of the flocks and herds."

Why would the Lord want to give us flocks and herds? Have you ever caught yourself reading a familiar passage and skipping over parts of it? I found myself doing that with this portion of the verse.

One day, while sharing this message at a conference in Mexico City, I paused and asked the Lord, "Lord, why do You want to bless us with flocks and herds?"

Though I have never heard the audible voice of the Lord, suddenly, I could see it all very clearly. How were the wealth and prosperity of a man measured in Bible times? By the amount of livestock he owned! Then I was able to understand that the Lord not only wants to supply our daily needs (the bread found in Zion), but He also wants to prosper and bless the dwellers of Zion.

Deuteronomy 28 says that He will open the storehouse of heaven to us and will abundantly bless us if we are obedient and keep His commandments (v. 12). What for? He continues, "You will lend to many nations...." The Lord's blessing on His people is always so they can bless others.

His blessing is never given to allow a person to live ostentatiously or to have great sums of money in the bank, since this draws attention away from God and to man. His purpose for blessing us is that we, in turn, can be a blessing to the nations of the earth.

God needs to free us from the mentality that promotes an ostentatious Christianity and teaches a false "prosperity." That message measures the "blessing" of the Lord by what kind of car a person drives or by $3,000 suits and expensive jewelry.

God wants to prosper us so that we can be a channel of blessing to many others and extend His kingdom on this earth. God wants to raise up prosperous businessmen to invest a lot of money in the kingdom of God in the whole earth. God is blessing us so that we may take His example and bless whenever we can. No wonder the Lord really likes Zion! It is a place of blessing, prosperity, and generosity. Who wouldn't like to live in a place like this?

5. Zion "... will be like a well-watered garden. ..." (Jer. 31:12).

Have you ever visited a garden right after it has been watered and enjoyed the wonderful smell of the water mixed in with the earth and the flowers? It smells fresh and clean. What a treat! What a delight!

This is how people who live in Zion "smell." They have a notable freshness of the Lord in their lives. They are not riddled with complexes and fears but are full of the Word of God. They emit a fragrant "odor" to all who come in contact with them. They bring freshness, energy, and an encouraging word when they enter a room.

By the same token, have you ever noticed how some people, when they enter a place, bring an ugly, stinking odor with them? Instead of encouragement, they bring a negative, pessimistic word. They doubt, question, and suspect everything. It is so disagreeable being around them! It is very likely that they are not citizens of Zion.

No wonder the Lord likes this place! Everyone smells good! Everyone has a beautiful, free, and encouraging spirit. There is a dynamic and exciting atmosphere about the Zion dweller—a refreshing and renewing attitude in all. It definitely sounds like the place I would like to live!

6. In Zion, "they will sorrow no more" (v. 12).

Wow! What more could we ask for? All our needs are met (bread), we have the joy of the Lord (wine), the fullness of His Spirit, healing for all our illnesses (oil), the blessing and prosperity with which to be generous to others (flocks and herds), the freshness of His Spirit (a watered garden), and also the promise of no more sorrow.

118

So many people go through life searching for "cures" for pain. I remember a neighborhood where we used to live in the city of Durango, Mexico. Trucks would go by, occasionally selling their magic powder that cures everything—toothaches, lack of energy, indigestion, pounding in your chest, hair falling out. Their cure was nothing more than ground-up rattlesnake rattles—the biggest hoax of all time.

Zion has the remedy of remedies: a solution for every ache and pain; a provision for every one of our hurts. It is no wonder the Lord chose this place to dwell in! Wouldn't you like to live in a neighborhood called Zion? It's where the Lord lives!

WHERE IS ZION?

ONE OF THE FIRST QUESTIONS I ASKED WHILE STUDYING ABOUT Zion was, *"Where* is this place the Bible calls Zion?" It is an actual place, such as the mountain named Zion in Israel. Do we actually have to go there to be able to experience all the things God says about living there? I think you already know the answer to this question: *no.* Then, where is this wonderful place where God dwells? The answer can be found in a verse we have read so often that we almost read it on autopilot:

> But You are holy,
> Enthroned in the praises of Israel.
> —PSALM 22:3, NKJV

There you have it! That is Zion! Each time you and I raise our hands and our voices in praise and acclamation to Him, we are building a Zion right there, a place in which He can dwell. Each time we raise our hearts to God in sincerity, love, and dedication, to exalt, proclaim, and honor His greatness and His power, we are constructing a Zion where He can descend in all His glory upon us.

He will bring all the things found in Zion: bread, wine, oil, prosperity, freshness, and freedom. This means that wherever you are, you can turn *that* place into a dwelling for the Lord. If you are washing the dinner plates, your kitchen can become a Zion. If you are driving your car to work, or riding the subway or some other form of public transportation to school, that place can become a Zion. The location doesn't matter; what matters is that the Lord is anxious for us to give Him a place where He can descend, dwell, and give us all the blessings promised to the inhabitants of Zion.

Use your imagination with me for a moment. I can see the Lord seated upon His throne, Michael at His left hand and Gabriel at His right. Suddenly, the Lord makes a sign with His hand that everyone already knows means "silence." The choir of angels stops singing, the heavenly musicians stop playing, and all becomes completely silent.

The Lord rises from His throne and looks over the balcony of heaven to see what is happening. You can tell He is listening to something. Gabriel and Michael look at each other out of the corner of their eyes, knowing what is going on because it has happened many times before.

You can barely catch the sound of a song: "Our God is an awesome God! He reigns from heaven above with wisdom, power, and love; our God is an awesome God!"[1]

The Lord leans over to Michael and asks, "Do you hear that?"

Michael answers, "Yes, it sounds lovely."

"Did you know those are My children?" the Lord asks.

"Yes, Lord; they are the ones You bought with Your precious blood."

The Lord continues listening to the song that has risen before Him, and a look of recognition crosses His face. "My child, how I love you," He whispers gently as He listens.

Having traveled all over Latin America, I have come to recognize the distinct expressions used in different countries. Certain expressions and cultural characteristics distinguish one Latin American country from one another.

It's the same with the "Zionite." There are certain expressions, attitudes, and customs that keep the "Zionite" separate from everyone else. Here are some of those characteristics:

1. Joy and gladness (Isa.51:3, 11; 35:10).
2. Singing and music (Isa. 51:3; Ps. 87:7).
3. Dancing (Jer. 31:13).
4. Everlasting joy (Isa. 35:10; 51:11).

Zionites love parties. They create an atmosphere; they know how to sing and give thanks in everything. They don't care what everyone else thinks about them. They only care what the Lord thinks about them. That is why they are often misunderstood, because some of the inhabitants of other dwellings can't understand why the Zionite is so boisterous.

I recall one Zionite who was savagely criticized because he had become "uncontrollable" in the presence of the Lord: King David. As he neared Jerusalem with the ark of the covenant in his possession, he was not able to contain his happiness and rejoicing. He began to dance with all his might in such a way that Michal, his wife, thought he was showing off before the king's maidservants.

There are "Michals" among us today who watch from their comfortable, secure balconies, far from involvement in worship, far from rejoicing with the Lord's people over the Lord's presence as it returns to where it belongs.

But Zionites don't care what the Michals say, because they know who they are doing it for and why they are doing it. Determination is another one of their characteristics. No matter what may be going on around them, the Zionite is always ready to praise and worship the great King of kings and Lord of lords.

It is interesting to note that David was the only person

God called a "man after my own heart" (Acts 13:22). How did this happen? Was it because God just had the notion to make him that? I don't believe so. I think that out there in the fields, while David watched his sheep with his harp in his hand, he began to experience God's presence within him. He discovered that spiritual "Zion" about which he wrote. He enjoyed intimate communion with the Lord and knew that each time he played his instrument and sang his songs, the Lord's presence descended.

No wonder David wrote so many beautiful psalms! No wonder he was the most powerful king of all times! He knew what it was to live in Zion! Don't you think it would be a wonderful place to live? Wouldn't you like to live in God's dwelling place? Then seek His presence. Lift up your worship, your thanksgiving, your praise, and your celebration before the throne of God, and He will descend and dwell with you. You will receive all the blessings that come from living in Zion.

We have a reason to sing . . .

> Sing, O Daughter of Zion;
>   shout aloud, O Israel!
> Be glad and rejoice with all your heart,
>   O Daughter of Jerusalem!
> The LORD has taken away your punishment,
>   he has turned back your enemy.
> The LORD, the King of Israel, is with you;
>   never again will you fear any harm.
> On that day they will say to Jerusalem,
>   "Do not fear, O Zion;
>   do not let your hands hang limp.
> The LORD your God is with you,
>   he is mighty to save.
> He will take great delight in you,
>   he will quiet you with his love,
>   he will rejoice over you with singing."
>   —ZEPHANIAH 3:14–17

Those Who Dwell in Zion

"Shout and be glad, O Daughter of Zion. For I am coming, and I will live among you," declares the LORD.

—ZECHARIAH 2:10

We have a very musical God—
He is the one who thought up the whole idea
of music. Let's begin using it for His glory
and exaltation just like it is done
"up there in heaven."

Nine

When We All Get to Heaven

THERE IS A HYMN WITH THE SAME TITLE AS THIS CHAPTER THAT we sang a lot as I was growing up. It seems that for a long time the church was caught in an "up-yonder" mentality—with little teaching about life "down here." As one person put it, there was a lot of singing about the "sweet by and by," and not much was said about the "gritty now and now."

> When we all get to heaven,
> What a day of rejoicing that will be!
> When we all see Jesus,
> We'll sing and shout the victory.[1]

When we see Jesus, there will be a lot of singing and shouting, that's for sure. If there is one thing that is clearly seen as we study the Book of Revelation, it is that there is an extraordinary amount of praise and worship

125

happening in heaven.

Because of this, I decided to take a short, simple journey through the entire book to see what I could find out about this praise and worship. Several interesting principles appeared, at which we will take a look. I believe that if we're going to be practicing these principles in heaven, it seems like a good idea to establish each of them in our lives now, before getting "up there."

THANKSGIVING, PRAISE, AND WORSHIP

FROM THE VERY BEGINNING OF THIS BOOK YOU ARE READING, we have established thanksgiving, praise, and worship as the main divisions for expressing our praise to God. In the Book of Revelation, we see each of these represented in heaven. I discovered this in a verse that I had read many times before: "Whenever the living creatures give glory, honor and thanks..." (Rev. 4:9). Here we find all three elements.

Let's take a look first at *thanks.* We have already discussed our need for firmly establishing this area of our lives. Gratitude is one of the characteristics of a true worshiper. How could there be ungrateful people in heaven? Can you imagine someone getting to heaven and complaining about the inadequacy of the facilities for meeting their needs? Perhaps complaining because the air conditioning doesn't work in their mansion? Impossible!

The official language of heaven will be praise and thanksgiving. Begin learning the language of gratitude right now; make it more than just a vocabulary—make it a lifestyle.

The second element of expression is *praise,* the second step in the protocol required to approach God. The word used in Revelation 4:9 is *honor.* Honor is practically synonymous with praise, since praise is simply recognizing the Lord's virtues and characteristics. To give honor is to praise His nature, His personality, and His character. It's acknowledging His qualities.

One way you can measure your acknowledgment of God is by looking around to see if you acknowledge your brothers and sisters. The apostle John writes that it is impossible to say we love God, whom we don't see, and hate our brother, whom we do see (1 John 4:20). The same thing is true in honoring God; how can we honor God, whom we don't see, and dishonor our brother, whom we do see?

We should be quick to acknowledge the virtues of fellow believers, pointing them out as we have opportunity.

The third thing we see in heaven is described by the word *glory*. There is a clear distinction between "honor" and "glory"—many can give honor to others, but we give glory to only one: He who lives for all eternity.

This same distinction can be seen between praise and worship. In praise we acknowledge and highlight the virtues of something or someone, but in worship we bow down in complete surrender to the rule of the King of kings and the Lord of lords. In contrast to thanks and honor, worship, or the giving of glory to God, is not something we practice here because we will also be doing it "up there"—if it *is not* practiced here, we *will not make it up there!*

Worship is a nonnegotiable, nonoptional part of our walk with the Lord. If we are not 100 percent surrendered to the lordship of Jesus Christ, we will never have the chance to sing with that choir of angels on the great final day, when every tongue, tribe, and nation will meet. If you are planning on going to heaven, it is urgent that you surrender your life to the lordship of Jesus Christ.

PROSTRATION

REVELATION 4:10 SAYS, "THE TWENTY-FOUR ELDERS FALL DOWN before him." Revelation 19:4 says, "The twenty-four elders and the four living creatures fell down and worshiped

God." This is the key to the worshiper the Father is seeking. Everyone in heaven bows before the throne. Besides the spiritual implication of prostration, I think it is important to learn to be physically prostrate as an outward sign of an inward decision. Many congregations don't practice prostration, even though it is one of the most biblical forms of expressing worship. I believe it would be good to reinstate it into our worship services.

There is something that happens in our heart when we kneel and bow before His Majesty. It is a good exercise for our flesh, just to remind it who is in control of our body. Occasionally, in a conference or other meeting, the Lord has led us to prostrate ourselves before Him. I cannot describe the feeling that comes over me when thousands of people bend their knees and bow before the great King as they pour out their hearts to Him. It is indescribable! Looking upon that kind of scene, I can almost imagine how it is going to be in heaven when we are all around the great throne, from which emanates the wonderful light of His presence. There we will bow, receiving the warmth of His love, prostrate with our crowns thrown at His feet. Let us begin to learn, right now, to bend our knee in humility before Him, acknowledging His great power and glory.

DECLARATIONS

THIS IS ANOTHER INTERESTING AREA OF WORSHIP THAT CAN BE found in the Book of Revelation. It is important to learn to use our mouths, tongues, and throats to declare eternal truths resoundingly to our enemy and also to our brother.

> Day and night they never stop saying:
> "Holy, holy, holy,
>   is the Lord God Almighty,
>   who was, and is, and is to come."
> —REVELATION 4:8

You are worthy, our Lord and God,
   to receive glory and honor and power.
                                    —REVELATION 4:11

In a loud voice they sang:
"Worthy is the Lamb, who was slain,
to receive power and wealth and wisdom and strength
and honor and glory and praise!"
                                    —REVELATION 5:12

And they cried out in a loud voice:
"Salvation belongs to our God,
who sits on the throne,
and to the Lamb."
                                    —REVELATION 7:10

These are just a few of the many declarations that were spoken throughout the entire revelation of the book.

We have heard messages many times about the power in the tongue to destroy and also to build up. James speaks about the tongue being an uncontrollable instrument that causes many problems for the whole world (James 3:8). How many times have we gotten into trouble because of a misguided word wrongly spoken or not thought out? One of the ways to strengthen our control over this area of our lives is by speaking only the Word of God. Each time we open our mouth, a blessing or powerful declaration from the Word should be coming out of it.

Revelation 12:11 says, "They overcame him by the blood of the Lamb and by the word of their testimony." What we speak, along with the work Jesus completed on the cross, will assure our victory. It is very important, then, to speak correctly! We must keep our tongue from speaking empty and profane words. We need to learn to speak and declare the only thing worth saying: The eternal Word of our Lord Jesus.

I think it is important to note from verse 11 the balance

between the blood of the Lamb and the word of testimony. Without the blood of the Lamb, the word of testimony would have been useless. The two things work in conjunction to bring us the victory. The blood of the Lamb has power, but it requires the word of testimony to *activate* the power. God's Word also tells us, "Heaven and earth will pass away, but my words will never pass away" (Matt. 24:35). If you want to speak eternal words, speak the Word of God. If you want to live in the victory already promised and purchased by Jesus, begin to declare it; put that victory in your mouth so it can invade the rest of your body. Speak it aloud so your entire being can hear your declaration and line up with the Word.

Declare the Word also to fellow believers. Many of the psalms are declarations of the Lord's greatness and reminders of His marvelous works. Take a moment to open the Book of Psalms, and you will see what I am talking about.

> Praise the LORD.
>
> —PSALM 134:1

> Praise the LORD.
> Praise, O servants of the LORD.
>
> —PSALM 113:1

> Come let us sing for joy to the LORD;
> let us shout aloud to the Rock of our salvation.
>
> —PSALM 95:1

These declarations are invitations to the church to exalt the virtues of our God together. Look for someone to whom you can declare a truth of the Word. We might as well know how to declare the Word here, because we will certainly be doing it "up there."

And declare the Word to the enemy. Revelation 12:11 says, "They overcame him..." Who is the "him"? It is the dragon, the serpent, the devil, Satan (v. 9). It is important to learn how to declare spiritual truths to the devil so they can be established according to the Word.

Many people are frightened of the devil, but according to the Word, he has been defeated by the victory Jesus obtained on the cross of Calvary. We need to remind our enemy of that victory every once in a while; we also need to remind ourselves. *Let's declare it!*

NOISE

AS I STUDIED WORSHIP AND PRAISE IN HEAVEN, I CAME ACROSS this point: There is a lot of noise going on there. Now, for those of us who don't like noise, there are a couple of suggestions I can think of:

1. Please do not go to heaven, because it is going to be very noisy up there.
2. If you insist on going to heaven, take some ear plugs if you do not like noise.
3. Do not read this section of the chapter, because we are going to justify the noise with Scripture.
4. (This is the best one.) Remember that we will have a new and glorified body, and the noise won't even be a problem!

Heaven is loud!

In a *loud* voice they sang...

—REVELATION 5:12

And they cried out in a *loud* voice...

—7:10

And I heard a sound from heaven like the *roar* of rushing waters and like a *loud* peal of thunder...

—14:2

I heard what sounded like the *roar* of a great multitude in heaven *shouting*...

—19:1

Then I heard what sounded like a great multitude, like the *roar* of rushing waters and like *loud* peals of thunder, *shouting*...

—19:6
—Italics added in previous verses for emphasis

None of these verses speak of silence—they speak of noise. Silence is not synonymous with spirituality. Silence is a biblical form of worship, but even silence, if used in extreme, can become idolatrous.

We have to learn to "be still, and know that [He is] God" (Ps. 46:10). We must learn to discern, value, and appreciate moments of silence in the presence of our Lord. Particularly in times of worship, there are the indispensable moments of silence. But, by the same token, we need to know how to make noise within the framework of praise.

Being disrespectful to God has nothing to do with noise level—it occurs with the attitude of the heart. If our heart is right with God, and we have a sincere desire to express what is in it, why not yell it to the four winds as they do in heaven? We yell and shout about so many other things—sports, social events, and musical concerts—why not shout and make known the fact that we have a great and wonderful God?

A few years ago, I was visiting the city of Toronto in Ontario, Canada, to minister in several Hispanic congregations there. One day, my host took me to visit Niagara Falls, a prospect that excited me since I had only seen the falls on postcards. It was rather late in the day when we went, and it began to get dark as we traveled.

"Brother, how much further is it? It looks like we won't make it before it gets dark," I said to my host.

He calmly answered, "Don't worry. It is going to be

even better at night. They turn on some big lights, and the falls look even more impressive."

This encouraged my wilting spirits. As we came near the falls, I started looking for the bright lights. My host was silent as he parked the car. "What about the lights?" I asked.

Rather soberly he answered, "Well…it looks as if they have turned them off already."

You cannot imagine my disappointment. I have only seen Niagara Falls *through the eyes of faith!*

Of course, the one thing I can say with total certainty is that I *heard* Niagara Falls. And what a sound! Never have I heard anything similar. As I stood at the guardrail by the valley of the river, I remembered the verse in Revelation about the roar of great waters. If you have never heard it, then it is quite an indescribable sound. I could imagine the time when we are gathered in heaven, praising the Lord with all our might, with all our voices, with all our beings—praise to the One who lives and reigns for all of time: "Holy, holy, holy, is the Lord God Almighty, who was, who is, and who is to come."

Can you imagine it with me? The time will be so incredible! And we can enjoy that time right here on earth. Let us be a people who give *supreme praise*—not a quiet, timid, mediocre little praise, but one given with all our might.

Musical Instruments

In the apostle John's vision of Revelation there are several references to musical instruments, especially to trumpets and harps:

> The twenty-four elders fell down before the Lamb.
> Each one had a harp.
>
> —5:8

Then the seven angels who had the seven trumpets

prepared to sound them.

—8:6

The sound I heard was like that of harpists playing their harps.

—14:2

Why were the harps given to the twenty-four elders? Were they just for show or just part of the heavenly decorations? Of course not! They were given the harps to play and praise the Lord. Many of us have been gifted by God to express ourselves on a musical instrument. It is important to use our giftings, since on that great final day, He will require an accounting of our musical gifts. It will be much better for us to have "invested" those talents, allowing them to grow and produce than to have done like the unfaithful servant in the parable of the talents (Matt. 25:14–30).

I am certain that many of us are unaware of all the talents God has given us. On judgment day, when we are required to give an account, we will discover talents we didn't even know we had. It is vital to look for and develop the talents the Lord has put in us, because, like the twenty-four elders with their harps, if it is there, it should be used to worship Him.

As a boy, my mother did everything possible to help her children discover the areas where we were gifted. For a short time, I studied drawing. After that, I took painting classes, and today, hanging in my mother's house is a collection of three original Marcos Witt paintings. Because of my mother's determination, my two brothers were found to be extraordinarily good artists and musicians; my sisters also developed their musical talents. My parents understood the biblical principle of talents and helped us to study as many different things as we possibly could. I can't imagine what would have happened if my parents had not insisted I study music. Maybe I would be waiting tables today!

Search your own life. Find out what kinds of aptitudes and talents in different areas you might have. Some day, the Lord will ask you, "Son, daughter, why did you never play the violin?"

To which you may answer, "Lord, I didn't know that I could play the violin."

The Lord will respond, "You didn't try either, did you?"

The music of heaven will accompany the declarations, praise, worship, and thanksgiving ascending before the throne. We have a very musical God—He is the one who thought up the whole idea of music. Let's begin using it for His glory and exaltation just like it is done "up there in heaven."

New Songs

And they sang a new song.

—5:9

And they sang a new song before the throne.

—14:3

[They] sang the song of Moses.

—15:3

This area of praise and worship really intrigues me because it is so different and beautiful; it can mean so much in the life of a believer. God gave me a burden several years ago to share more about the new song, because I believe more of us should be singing it.

When you hear the term *new song,* there are several ways to look at it:

- Simply that…a new song that has never been sung before
- A new song especially for you
- A spontaneous song

- A prophetic song

A newly composed song

In these times when the Lord is restoring praise and worship to many of us, it is wonderful to see the extraordinary number of new songs coming from all parts of the world. I feel privileged to be a part of the group of new composers God has raised up in our Latin American world. Most of the songs being written today not only have great musical beauty but wonderful content, too. I believe it is so important that our songs have lots of the Word in them. We need songs that declare the eternal truths established in the everlasting, infallible Word of God. Singing a new song is like eating a slice of bread fresh out of the oven with plenty of melted butter on it. A new song can elevate the praise and worship to new levels, requiring that we think about the lyrics. A song with the fresh, living anointing of the Holy Spirit can break yokes and bring brokenness, liberty, and healing to God's people.

Introduce new songs to your congregation. Find projects produced by many different ministries, and bring the freshness of these songs to your congregations. However, be careful not to overdo it, bombarding the congregation with so many new songs they aren't able to digest them.

Ask the Lord to give you songs of your own—don't just sing the songs recorded by others.

A new song for you

A song does not have to be newly composed to be a new song for you. Many people have never heard the old hymns; many others have never heard the new songs. Both groups need to find a good middle ground; there are songs on both sides that can edify, teach, and motivate others.

The Lord laid it on my heart some time ago to do a recording with some of the old hymns on it. We recorded some of the hymns I sang growing up, arranged in a contemporary style to offer this generation of young people some of the great songs that make up a part of our Christian heritage. I believe in the hymns and have made a positive effort to revive them among this new generation of believers.

I invite those who love old hymns and those who love new songs to seek out the songs that are "new" to them.

Spontaneous songs

One of the best examples I have found to explain spontaneous songs is my children. After all, the Lord said, "From the lips of children and infants you have ordained praise" (Matt. 21:16). We can find many examples of praise and worship in our children. Many times children will begin to sing a "song" that has no rhyme, reason, direction, or defined theme. But they sing as if it were one of the oldest songs on record. They sing about the birds they see flying by, the cows in the field, or how wonderful their mommy and daddy are. This is a new song—something that expresses what the child is feeling. These spontaneous songs must affect the heart of God much like a specially chosen greeting card touches the heart of a parent. Most of us, at one time or another, have had to make a card for our mother on Mother's Day. We took a sheet of paper and some crayons and crafted a very special "card" for our mother. Works of art they were not! Underneath the artwork we wrote our special thoughts: *Mom, you are the prettiest one in the whole world. I love you lots and lots.*

Every mother received that little "card" as if it were as priceless as an heirloom oil painting. Why? Because it was the authentic, spontaneous expression of love from a child. She is moved by the feelings in her child's heart. It is the same with our spontaneous "new songs" to the Lord. They may be out of sync and out of tune musically speaking, but they are a little personalized "card" that we can offer to the Lord to describe what we are feeling in our heart for Him.

In Exodus 15 we find a wonderful example of "the song of Moses." After living for centuries in slavery, the Lord sent Moses to liberate the people of Israel from under the heavy hand of the Egyptian pharaoh. Most of us know the story of how God hardened Pharaoh's heart and had to deal severely with him to get him to let Israel go. After losing his firstborn son, Pharaoh finally let them go. But after two or three days he changed his mind and pursued them.

Meanwhile, Moses and the people had arrived at the Red Sea, but they had no way of getting to the other side—the sea loomed in front of them, and they were closed in by mountains on both sides.

God gives Moses a plan: Extend the rod, and He would take care of everything else. With the entire nation of Israel looking on, God divided the Red Sea, dried the land, and the Israelites crossed over on dry ground. But from the other side, they turned around and saw that Pharaoh was crossing, with his army right behind him, on the same dry ground God had prepared for His people.

But all of a sudden, *whoosh!* God closed up the walls of water in the sea and buried Pharaoh and his entire army. Right before their eyes, God freed them from Egypt's slavery in a spectacular way!

Can you imagine how they all felt? I imagine that for about three or four minutes there was complete, incredulous silence. Then one by one the people began to sing until there was an unbearably loud noise of rejoicing, celebration, and shouts of jubilee. (See Exodus 15:1–21.)

I believe Moses, along with the people, was shouting with joy, celebrating this great victory. At that moment, what kind of song would be appropriate? Of all the songs, hymns, and psalms that existed, which one could be sung to express the specific kind of joy they were feeling at that moment? NONE! They needed to make up a new one, one to describe the feelings in their heart and the circumstances at that precise moment. This is the same way that "spiritual songs" allow us to sing spontaneously in order to express what no other song or hymn could describe. Give this type of expression a place in your personal and congregational life.

Prophetic songs

This aspect of the "new song" carries a dimension that we haven't tapped into yet. This is the song that the Lord sings to us, His people. The Bible calls it the "song of the LORD" (2 Chron. 29:27, NKJV). Psalm 42:8 simply calls it "his song."

Many passages in the Bible refer to our God's singing. The most beautiful one is found in Zephaniah 3:17:

> The LORD your God is with you,
>   he is mighty to save.
> He will take great delight in you,
>   he will quiet you with his love,
>   he will rejoice over you with singing.

I believe with all my heart that the Lord has many songs to teach and exhort us by way of the prophetic song. The Lord wants to sing prophetically through us, revealing His plans, thoughts, and character to us.

One of the passages that most strongly supports the fact of God speaking through song is found in Deuteronomy 31:

> Now write down for yourselves this song and teach it to the Israelites and have them sing it, so that it may be a witness for me against them....So Moses wrote down this song that day and taught it to the

139

Israelites.... And Moses recited the words of this song from the beginning to end in the hearing of the whole assembly of Israel.

—DEUTERONOMY 31:19, 22, 30

This song is recorded in Deuteronomy 32. It is a perfect example of a prophetic song. In the Psalms, many of the songs are sung by the Lord *for us*. These are prophetic songs. We need to learn more about this so we can practice it within the body of Christ.

Music, singing, and praising all have something in common—the prophetic realm contained therein. Music and song help to loose the prophetic word of God. (See 2 Kings 3:15.) Let's learn how to sing the prophetic song.

This chapter has shown us a few of the things we can expect "up there in heaven." Did you see yourself singing and worshiping in heaven as you read these passages? Have you realized that John saw you and me there? It's never too late. If you still have not learned how to be a true worshiper, now is when you should make the commitment, because once you get up there, you won't have the chance to learn.

Are you making your plans to be "up there" with us? Since you are, get ready to make lots of music with new songs, strong and noisy declarations, thanksgiving, honor, and glory. And don't forget the most important characteristic to get there: Keep your life bowed before the throne of God, and allow Him to be the only One to reign and govern your life always.

Are you willing to do that? Then you have just taken another important step to becoming a true worshiper.

Let's control our emotions in such a way
that it makes the experience of corporate
worship a pleasant one, not only for us,
but for the people around us as well.

Ten

Common Problems
in Praise and Worship

I N THIS SECTION WE WILL ANALYZE SOME OF THE IMPEDIMENTS
most frequently found in the lives of people who
desire to enter a deeper dimension of praise and worship.
I have become aware that in most cases these erroneous
ideas are due simply to a lack of understanding (Hos.
4:6). Once we get these ideas out into the light of His Word,
realizing the potential they have for causing problems in
our lives, we can come against them forcibly; in that way
we come closer to our goal of becoming "true worshipers."

It's a shame that so many have allowed some of these
wrong concepts to keep them from enjoying the fullness
of the blessings that come from living in Zion (a true
worshiper).

"I DON'T FEEL LIKE WORSHIPING"

I HAVE HEARD THIS PHRASE OFTEN OVER THE YEARS FROM PEOPLE

who think that if they don't feel like worshiping the Lord, then they are exempt from it. They base this belief on the idea that if it "doesn't come naturally," then there would be a lack of sincerity. Therefore, they shouldn't worship the Lord.

We don't praise and worship the Lord because we *feel like it*. We praise Him because of the eternal and fundamental fact that *He is worthy* to be praised, regardless of how we may feel. To become a true worshiper, it is necessary for us to establish this precept in our own worship life. Then we will be able to give Him glory under any circumstance, no matter what the situation may be, because we acknowledge that He is God and worthy to receive praise.

Those of us who are parents can understand this concept a little better. We love our children, not because they never give us any problems or are always obedient, but simply because they are ours. It is the same with the Lord. Our love for Him should not be based on our feelings but on the powerful fact that He is worthy.

The important role of obedience is lost in this mentality of "I don't feel like worshiping." The Lord commands us, hundreds of times, in the Bible to praise and worship Him. Why, then, do we "reserve the right" to worship Him only when we feel like it? Don't we understand that one of the things that pleases God is His children's obedience?

How can we call Him *Lord* if we are not willing to obey Him in everything, including praising and worshiping Him? The word *Lord* means "owner, ultimate authority, boss." How is it that we call Him "boss" and "ultimate authority," but we give Him praise only when we feel like it? This cannot be. We need to make some adjustments in this area of our Christian life; it is better to obey than to do what we think should be done.

As a child, I recall my mother sending me to the store to buy milk and bread, a ritual that took place almost every afternoon. I can't tell you exactly how many times the performing of this duty did "not come naturally" to me, but I'm sure it was somewhere in the neighborhood of 1,337 times. I never allowed the words "I don't feel like it" to come out of my mouth—the consequences would have been severe.

There are many things we do out of pure obedience. For example, I don't know of a single person who gets up in the morning, smiles at his reflection in the mirror while brushing his hair, and in a joyful, happy voice says, "Today I am going to pay the electric bill, because I feel like doing it." We wait to pay those bills until the last possible moment, precisely because it is not something that comes "naturally" to us—however, we pay it, don't we?

In the same way, when it comes to praise and worship, we do it because He is worthy and because we are obedient to His commandments. Let us consider some of these commands for a moment. They are not "recommendations" the Lord has made; they are not "options"— they are very clear orders that the Lord expects to be obeyed.

Sing praises to the LORD, enthroned in Zion;
    proclaim among the nations what he has done.
                              —PSALM 9:11

Ascribe to the LORD, O mighty ones,
    ascribe to the LORD glory and strength.
Ascribe to the LORD the glory due his name;
    worship the LORD in the splendor of his holiness.
                            —PSALM 29:1–2

Sing to the LORD, you saints of his;
    praise his holy name.
                            —PSALM 30:4

Love the LORD, all his saints!
                            —PSALM 31:23

Sing joyfully to the LORD, you righteous;
   it is fitting for the upright to praise him.
Praise the LORD with the harp;
   make music to him on the ten-stringed lyre.
Sing to him a new song;
   play skillfully, and shout for joy.

—PSALM 33:1–3

Shout with joy to God, all the earth!
   Sing the glory of his name;
   make his praise glorious!
Say to God, "How awesome are your deeds…"

Come and see what God has done,
   how awesome his works in man's behalf…
Praise our God, O peoples,
   let the sound of his praise be heard.

—PSALM 66:1–3, 5, 8

Sing to God, sing praise to his name,
   extol him who rides on the clouds—
his name is the LORD—
   and rejoice before him.

—PSALM 68:4

Sing for joy to God our strength;
   shout aloud to the God of Jacob!
Begin the music, strike the tambourine,
   play the melodious harp and lyre.

Sound the ram's horn at the New Moon,
   and when the moon is full, on the day of our Feast;
this is a decree for Israel,
   an ordinance of the God of Jacob.

—PSALM 81:1–4

You may be thinking that this is a cold, impersonal way

to worship the Lord—doing it solely out of obedience. As we mentioned earlier, the Lord is seeking worshipers who worship "in spirit and in truth" (John 4:24).

We need to learn how to be "spiritual" Christians, allowing our spirit to be in control of all the areas of our life, because man's spirit is where God's Spirit dwells. They communicate and relate to one other, or at least they should.

Paul advised us to be spiritual, not carnal Christians (1 Cor. 3:1–3). He understood that if our spirit is in control of our life, then very probably that meant the Lord is in control; but if our flesh is in control, we are simply carnal Christians.

There is an interesting passage of Scripture found in Romans that presents us with the problem of the flesh versus the spirit, a problem that we all have from the first day we enter the kingdom of God. (See Romans 5–8.)

There is a constant struggle between these two forces in our lives. Who will win? The answer is simple: Whoever is stronger in us, and whoever receives more nourishment will be the winner. If we feed the spirit more, then it will win the battles that we have against sin and our flesh. If we feed our flesh more, then it will win the victories.

The same law applies to the struggle to become true worshipers. We have to allow our spirit, who is always willing, to lead our praise and worship to the Lord—not our flesh, because our flesh will never "want" to praise and worship.

The psalmist David helped us to find a solution to the problem when he wrote Psalm 103:1: "Praise the LORD, O my soul; all my inmost being, praise his holy name." The whole problem is resolved in these few words.

We can find all three parts of our being in this psalm: Spirit, soul, and body. The soul is easy to find, because it is clearly mentioned: "Praise the LORD, O my soul." The body is indicated by the words "all my inmost being."

But, where is the spirit found in this scripture? It is the one giving the orders! At this point, the psalmist understands that the only way his body and soul are going to worship is as his spirit, full of the Holy Spirit, gives them the order to do it. Otherwise "it won't come naturally"; they won't "feel like it."

David would not allow his body (flesh)—that independent, rebellious, and stubborn part of his being—to dictate when to praise the Lord. In the same way, he did not allow something as vulnerable, indecisive, and fickle as his soul to tell him when to worship God. Instead, he put the matter into his spirit's hands, who, having a relationship with God's Spirit, told the other two (body and soul) when it was time to praise the Lord.

It's no wonder David could say, "I will extol the LORD at all times; his praise will always be on my lips" (Ps. 34:1). His spirit was always in control of his worship, not his soul or body.

THE EMOTIONAL PROBLEM

GOD GAVE US EMOTIONS FOR A SPECIAL PURPOSE, AND WE CAN enjoy them in many ways. God has not given us emotions to govern and control our life, but to bring richness to it. We have all seen people who allow their emotions to control their lives. We have all been in a service when suddenly a precious brother or sister begins to feel such a strong emotion that he or she expresses it openly and at full volume.

As a boy, I remember visiting my grandfather's church in the United States. There was a sister in his congregation who always, at the high point of worship, stood up, began turning in circles, and shouted at the top of her lungs. It would leave all the kids under fifteen years of age totally spooked. Especially those who had never experienced it before.

Upon seeing her "get blessed" (that's what this activity

was commonly called), another two or three brothers and sisters would suddenly feel the "blessing." Before you knew it, a choir of four or five people were shouting, spinning around, and doing some pretty strange things while everyone else watched. Some were surprised, others were bored (because they saw it in every service), and others like myself were scared to the bone.

What was all this about? I believe that it was a lack of understanding on how to correctly channel the strong emotions we experience upon being in the Lord's presence. Not knowing what to do, they provided a very interesting spectacle to the people around them, with shouts and expressions they believed were characteristic of a spiritual person.

Their intentions were correct, and without a doubt they were feeling something. But many times, such unharnessed emotions have impeded our flowing together as one body with one spirit in that time of corporate worship.

Paul had to write to the Corinthians to straighten out some problems related to church order. (See 1 Corinthians 12–14.) Paul taught that it is very important that everything be done "in a fitting and orderly way" during a corporate gathering (14:40).

Paul doesn't speak about how to worship in your private time with the Lord. You can do whatever you want to there, but in the gathering together as a group of believers, we need to learn how to be a "spiritual" worshiper and not an emotional one.

There will be a time for everything in a praise and worship service. Even when we gather together as a body of believers, almost always there is a time to express nearly every emotion we may have. We should take advantage of these times and flow with the rest of the body so that all will be edified and blessed together. When one individual has an emotional display during a corporate gathering, they are not being sensitive to the rest of the body. The emotional believer has not yet learned that the spirit of the prophet is subject to the prophet (1 Cor. 14:32). We have been given a spirit of self-discipline by God (2 Tim. 1:7).

Let me encourage you that when it's time to shout— let's shout! When it's time to clap our hands—let's all clap! When it is time to keep silent—let's all be silent! Let's flow as one body, the body of Christ that we are. Let's control our emotions in such a way that it makes the experience of corporate worship a pleasant one, not only for us, but for the people around us as well.

"SOMETHING KEEPS ME FROM WORSHIPING"

I'VE HEARD MANY SINCERE PEOPLE SAY THIS. USUALLY THEY'RE people who want to enter into a deeper dimension in their worship life, but they feel that the more they struggle and try, the less successful they are at reaching their objective.

Several verses in the Bible show us some reasons why these persons are struggling to become true worshipers:

Prisons

"Set me free from my prison, that I may praise your name" (Ps. 142:7). Many people find themselves bound in different kinds of prisons. Some are in the prison of complexes and lies that they have believed about themselves all of their lives. Perhaps someone belittled or mistreated them for a long time, and they have not been able to get over this treatment. It has turned into an inferiority complex or simply a general unhappiness with life. The Lord can tear down this prison in our lives.

Another prison can exist in the form of religion or religious customs. It is very difficult for some people to change the way they do things simply because they have been doing it that way for years. Their expressions of worship have become habits or traditions—they are no longer an expression of the heart.

I often hear the phrase, "But we have never done it that way in our church; it isn't our custom." Because of that "custom," individuals have missed out on some of the blessings the Lord has in store for those who will praise and worship Him wholeheartedly. This is one of the most common prisons among people today because religious customs allow a certain air of "spirituality" to be feigned, thus fooling those who are close to us and making them think we are very spiritual persons. Watch out for religious customs! They have bound many people, keeping them from becoming true worshipers.

Another common prison is fear. Fear of failure, fear of simply not doing something, or fear of offending God. There are thousands of fears that weigh people down, keeping them from becoming true worshipers. There are some who even fear not being received by the Lord. It must be terrible to live in this state of mind! We have to get rid of all these fears in order to enter that deeper dimension of worship the Lord wants us to enter. Fill up on the Word; it will fill you with the knowledge of God's love, and that is the perfect love that will drive out fear (1 John 4:18).

If you desire to worship on a deeper, more committed level, but you've felt some resistance, look at your life in the light of the Word of God to see if there is a prison that has prevented or made it nearly impossible to move ahead on the road to true worship. Jesus came to break all the chains and liberate the captives. When we are hidden in Him, we don't have to keep on living in those prisons. Be free to worship Him, in Jesus' name!

> He found the place where it was written: "The Spirit of the Lord is on me, because he has anointed me to preach good news to the poor. He has sent me to proclaim freedom for the prisoners and recovery of sight for the blind, to release the oppressed, to proclaim the year of the Lord's favor." Then...he began by

saying to them, "Today this scripture is fulfilled in your hearing."

—LUKE 4:17–21

Lack of Teaching

Psalm 119:171 says, "May my lips overflow with praise, for you teach me your decrees." Many of us simply feel disabled by our lack of understanding on the subject of praise. There is so much that we need to learn on the subject. It should be a lifelong journey. We should ask the Lord on a daily basis to show us more and more about how to become true worshipers. I encourage you to keep studying everything you can find in the Bible on this subject so that you can be well founded and knowledgeable.

Don't let your lack of knowledge keep you from becoming a true worshiper.

Death

Psalm 115:17 says, "It is not the dead who praise the LORD, those who go down to silence." That is obvious when speaking of physical death, but what about the thousands of believers who are dying spiritually? They can't praise Him because they are not alive to Him. They are doing things out of custom or habit—the closest thing there is to spiritual death. They think that by fulfilling a religious ritual and going to a service once in a while, they're going to be okay with God; they don't know that their heart is far from Him.

These people may question another person's exuberant praises by saying, "Oh well, they're new—they'll get over it." What an extraordinary example of spiritual death!

A dead person feels nothing, gets excited about nothing, gets happy about nothing—he simply has no feeling; he is dead. If you have some of those symptoms, check yourself out and see if there is a need to resurrect your spiritual life. The best way to be resurrected is to die to self and be resurrected into the life of Jesus Christ.

Take some time and renew your commitment right now. Don't go on until you have taken care of anything that may be keeping you from becoming a true worshiper.

PRIDE

ANOTHER COMMON OBSTACLE IN THE LIFE OF THE CHRISTIAN WHO wants to become a true worshiper, but for some reason is not able to do it, is the spirit of pride that can enter our life. We all battle against pride. Our flesh always has the desire to be seen, acknowledged, praised, raised up, and everything else that has to do with gratifying it. Some seem to have learned how to hide their pride better than others, but they live in a constant state of deceit, with a great need for the Lord to break them and do away with all the junk inside of them. A very good friend of mine told me once, "When God breaks us, He doesn't do it to destroy us, but to destroy the incorrect attitudes in our lives so that His glory can be reflected through us."

What a powerful truth! What a true principle!

Part of being a true worshiper is humbling ourselves before Him, acknowledging that "He is all...I am nothing (without Him)." The very *essence* of worship (prostration) is humility. How can we be a true worshiper without showing absolute humility before Him? It is impossible! Pride has kept many from receiving the blessings the Lord has prepared for those who will dare to praise and worship Him with all their might.

Many are very concerned about what the people who are watching them will think. "I won't be able to raise my hands...what will people say?" "I won't be able to shout with a voice of triumph...what will they say?" "I might lose the prestige I have worked so hard to obtain if I start dancing with everyone else. I think I'll just stand here, without moving, cold and indifferent to the Lord's commandments; I'm a very respected individual, and I don't want to tarnish my image for anything in the world."

Are you more interested in pleasing Him, yourself, or others? If you don't want to please Him, it is going to be very difficult for you to become a true worshiper. Paul writes: "Am I now trying to win the approval of men, or of God? Or am I trying to please men? If I were still trying to please men, I would not be a servant of Christ" (Gal. 1:10). It could not be any clearer. If we are wanting to please men, we simply are not servants of Christ. Those who serve Christ are characterized by their humility and desire to please Him.

The Pharisees were so "spiritual" that it was impossible for them to be humble. They were a perfect picture of pride. They considered themselves to be the epitome of spirituality, and yet they were so far from God. They must have thought to themselves: *How can someone be humble when they possess so many extraordinary spiritual characteristics?* The Pharisees are the same men who always wanted to halt praise of Jesus. At every opportunity, they tried to keep the people from praising God:

> When he came near the place where the road goes down the Mount of Olives, the whole crowd of disciples began joyfully to praise God in loud voices for all the miracles they had seen: "Blessed is the king who comes in the name of the Lord!" "Peace in heaven and glory in the highest!"
>
> Some of the Pharisees in the crowd said to Jesus, "Teacher, rebuke your disciples!"
>
> "I tell you," he replied, "if they keep quiet, the stones will cry out."
>
> —LUKE 19:37–40

The blind and the lame came to him at the temple, and he healed them. But when the chief priests and

the teachers of the law saw the wonderful things he
did and the children shouting in the temple area,
"Hosanna to the Son of David," they were indignant.
—MATTHEW 21:14–15

There are still Pharisees among us today! People who
would rather kill the Lord (it was the Pharisees who
sought Jesus' death and were finally successful in killing
Him) than allow others to acclaim and praise Him.

Beware of this spirit; don't allow it to control you!
Make sure there are no traces of a pharisaical spirit in
you. And if there are, destroy them in the name of Jesus,
so you can go on in the quest to become a true worshiper.

"AUTOPILOT" ATTITUDES

THIS IS ANOTHER PROBLEM COMMONLY FACED AMONG THOSE WHO
want to worship the Lord better. As humans, we have the
tendency to do things out of habit and custom. During
praise and worship, many times we sing the same songs
over and over on "autopilot." In other words, we're not
even thinking about what we're singing. We just do it
automatically.

It is so important that each time we raise our voice to
give Him glory and honor, we do it as if it were the very
first time. Take care not to be an "autopilot" worshiper,
but always think about what you're singing or saying to
the Lord, making it real for yourself and making it a daily
practice in your life.

Here are some early warning signs of being on "autopilot":

1. While worshiping and singing, you notice that
   Sister Susie has a new hairdo (and in your
   opinion, it isn't very attractive).

2. While worshiping, bowed down, you notice that

the carpet is worn out, and your eyes follow the worn-out trail, all without missing a beat of what is being sung.

3. With your eyes turned upward and your hands raised, you count all the ceiling tiles as you sing.

4. During the time of celebration, you work out the solution to a problem at work without missing a beat as you clap.

These are only a few of the warning signs of needing a renewal in your worship life. While we are praising and worshiping, we need to give God our complete attention, allowing Him to work in our life through the praise and the worship.

Don't let anything or anyone keep you from receiving *everything* the Lord has prepared for you through the wonderful experience of praise and worship.

*T*o worship God
is to embrace
the whole truth
of God.
To worship God
is to obey
the whole counsel
of God.

Conclusion

Heart of worship

OF EVERYTHING WE STUDIED IN THIS BOOK, WHAT I WOULD want to be indelibly written on your heart is that praise and worship is not singing or playing pretty music or having a Sunday morning program—it is a way of living and a condition of the heart.

The Lord is seeking an intimate relationship with us. He desires to have a friendship with each one of His children. For that to take place, we must give Him all. It can be summed up in the following phrase: To worship God is to embrace the whole truth of God. To worship God is to obey the whole counsel of God.

I hope that you will now have the desire and the understanding to become a better and truer worshiper. It is simple: Surrender to Him in every area, and you will be closer to becoming a true worshiper. So, let's live a worship-filled life!

—MARCOS WITT

Notes

Chapter Two
Praise

1. Don McMinn, *The Practice of Praise* (Nashville, TN: Word Music, 1992), n.p.
2. Terry Law, *The Power of Praise and Worship* (Tulsa, OK: Victory House, Inc., 1985), n.p.
3. *"Majestuoso, Poderoso"* by Fermín García. Copyright © 1988 by CanZion Producciones. All rights reserved. Used by permission.

Chapter Five
Why Is There a Shortage of Worshipers?

1. *New Bible Dictionary* (Wheaton, IL: Intervarsity Press, 1994), s.v. "throne."

Chapter Six
An Encounter With God

1. "Change My Heart, Oh God" by Eddie Espinosa. Copyright © 1982, Mercy/Vineyard Publishing (admin. by Music Services). All rights reserved. Used by permission.

Chapter Eight
Those Who Dwell in Zion

1. "Awesome God" by Rich Mullins. Copyright © 1988 BMG Songs, Inc. (ASCAP). All rights reserved. Used by permission.

Chapter Nine
When We All Get to Heaven

1. "When We All Get to Heaven" by Eliza E. Hewitt Public domain.

About the Author

Born on May 19, 1962 in San Antionio, Texas, to a missionary family, Marcos Witt was raised in Durango, Mexico. He was taught music from an early age.

In 1987, disillusioned with the status of Spanish Christian music, Witt started CanZion Producciones, a music production company. Today CanZion has offices in Durango and Houston, with international distribution. Witt has become the best-known Spanish Christian musician, with well over one million albums sold. Some of his concerts are attended by more than fifty thousand people at a time.

However, Witt's ministry transcends the boundaries of music and has also become an apostolic ministry. His concerts are truly an evangelistic effort where many receive salvation, healing, and deliverance. He has founded a Christian university in Durango where students are taught not only music skills but also theology and biblical studies. There are plans for a second campus to open in Houston.

Marcos married Miriam on March 1, 1986, and they have four children.

TO CONTACT MARCOS WITT OR FOR MORE
INFORMATION ON CANZION PRODUCCIONES:

CANZION—USA

914 N. Greens Rd., Suite 2
Houston, TX 77067
PHONE: (281) 873-5080
FAX: (281) 873-5084

CANZION—MEXICO

Campanilla No. 34
Fracc. Jardines de Durango
Durango, Durango 34200 MEXICO
PHONE: (011) 521-817-2464
FAX: (011) 521-818-1-0779

WEB SITE: \\www.canzion.com